Anatomy of a False Confession

Anatomy of a False Confession

The Interrogation and Conviction of Brendan Dassey

Michael D. Cicchini

Rowman & Littlefield
Lanham • Boulder • New York • London

Published by Rowman & Littlefield
A wholly owned subsidary of The Rowman & Littlefield Publishing Group, Inc.
4501 Forbes Boulevard, Suite 200, Lanham, Maryland 20706
www.rowman.com

Unit A, Whitacre Mews, 26-34 Stannary Street, London SE11 4AB

British Library Cataloguing in Publication Information Available

Library of Congress Cataloging-in-Publication Data

Names: Cicchini, Michael D., 1967- , author.
Title: Anatomy of a false confession : the interrogation and conviction of
  Brendan Dassey / Michael D. Cicchini JD.
Description: Lanham : Rowman & Littlefield, 2018. | Includes bibliographical
  references.
Identifiers: LCCN 2018022462 (print) | LCCN 2018026513 (ebook) | ISBN
  9781538117163 (Electronic) | ISBN 9781538117156 (cloth : alk. paper)
Subjects: LCSH: Dassey, Brendan--Trials, litigation, etc. | Trials
  (Murder)--Wisconsin. | Confession (Law)--United States. | Police
  questioning--United States. | Judicial error--United States.
Classification: LCC KF225.D37 (ebook) | LCC KF225.D37 C53 2018 (print) | DDC
  345.775/02523--dc23
LC record available at https://lccn.loc.gov/2018022462

$\infty^{\text{™}}$ The paper used in this publication meets the minimum requirements of
American National Standard for Information Sciences—Permanence of Paper
for Printed Library Materials, ANSI/NISO Z39.48-1992.

Printed in the United States of America

CONTENTS

CONTENTS

DISCLAIMERS

First, this book has not been written, published, approved, licensed, or sponsored by any person or entity that created or produced the Netflix documentary *Making a Murderer*. This book is an independent and unauthorized exploration of the legal, evidentiary, and ethical issues in the court cases of *State v. Dassey*, *Dassey v. Dittmann*, and *State v. Avery*.

Second, this book is not legal advice. This book should not be used for legal research or for any purpose other than entertainment and enjoyment. The author and the publisher are not responsible for any actions taken, or decisions made, by the readers of this book. Reading this book, or even contacting the author, does not create an attorney-client relationship. If you have legal questions or legal issues of any kind, immediately call a licensed attorney in your state.

Third, the author and the publisher do not endorse, or guarantee the accuracy of, the source documents cited in this book.

Part I

FALSE CONFESSION BASICS

I

BRENDAN DASSEY'S CONFESSION

By most accounts, Brendan Dassey was a quiet, shy, learning-disabled, sixteen-year-old kid with a low IQ score and bad grades. When he wasn't in school, he liked to play videogames and watch professional wrestling. Granted, he wasn't setting the world on fire, but neither was he causing any problems. He had never been in any trouble or even had any meaningful police contacts before October 31, 2005, the day that Teresa Halbach disappeared after visiting Steven Avery's property to photograph a vehicle.

As viewers of *Making a Murderer* know, Halbach's body was eventually found on Avery's property; she had been shot in the head and her corpse was burned. There was no physical evidence or eyewitnesses that linked Dassey to the crime. Yet within a few months, Dassey confessed that he and his uncle Steven had raped and murdered the victim and then placed her body in the fire.

It's not easy to figure out exactly what Dassey confessed to doing. It's harder still to determine when he confessed to doing it. Dassey was interrogated by detectives multiple times, including on November 6, 2005, in the back of a squad car; on February 27, 2006, at Mishicot High School; again on February 27 at the Two Rivers Police Department; later still on February 27 at a hotel; on March 1 at the Manitowoc County Sheriff's Department; and on May 13 at the Sheboygan County Law Enforcement Center. All of these interrogations, except for the questioning at the hotel, were either audio or video recorded and are cited in this book.[1]

The version of the confession that the state used to convict Dassey is roughly as follows.[2] On Halloween of 2005, the day Halbach disappeared, Dassey had been in school. When his school bus dropped him off, he started to walk up the road toward his home—one of several trailers on the Avery property. As he was walking, he looked over to his Uncle Steven's trailer and saw Halbach's jeep-like vehicle, a RAV4, parked in the garage. Halbach and Avery were nowhere to be seen. Dassey went home, but a short time later came back outside. And that's when he heard screams coming from inside Avery's trailer.

Dassey approached the trailer and knocked on the door. It took a while, but his Uncle Steven answered and invited him in. As prosecutor Ken Kratz enjoyed saying, Avery was all "sweaty" and "full of sweat."[3] Avery informed Dassey that he had Halbach chained up in his bedroom and was in the middle of raping her. He invited Dassey to join in the crime, and the two of them discussed their next steps over a soda in Avery's kitchen.

After Dassey drank his beverage, the two went back into Avery's bedroom where Dassey saw Halbach, restrained on the bed, still pleading to be released. The sixteen-year-old boy, who had never had sex before, accepted Avery's invitation to sexually assault the prisoner. Avery watched, and when Dassey was through, he congratulated him, telling the boy "that's how you do it."

Once the sexual assault was completed, the two adjourned to another room where they watched a little television and mulled over their next move. Soon thereafter, Avery got a knife and stabbed Halbach in the stomach; he then gave the knife to Dassey who cut her throat. However, Halbach survived, so Avery manually strangled her. But Halbach still wouldn't die, so they carried her out of the now-bloody trailer and into the garage. Because she survived the stabbing, throat slashing, and manual strangulation, Avery ramped up his efforts: he got his rifle and shot her "ten times," Dassey said, finally putting her out of her misery.

Avery and Dassey then put Halbach's body in the back of her RAV4, but only temporarily. They soon took her body out of the vehicle and put it in the bonfire that Avery had already started before Dassey arrived. To dispose of Halbach's car, they drove it to the very edge of the Avery property and placed it high up on a ridge. At that time, Avery went under the hood of the SUV for reasons unknown to Dassey. The two then placed some tree branches on the vehicle in a half-hearted attempt to conceal it.

Avery and Dassey walked back to the scene of the crime where they cleaned up the garage and burned Halbach's clothing. At this time, Dassey also saw that Avery had placed the contents of Halbach's purse—or at least her camera and cell phone—into a nearby burn barrel. The two then went inside Avery's trailer where Avery put Halbach's now-famous RAV4 key into his dresser drawer.

According to the state, Dassey had no problem living with his crimes—at least for a while. But eventually the guilt gnawed away at him. His young relative, Kayla Avery, told investigator Mark Wiegert that Dassey was crying a lot and had lost weight. This pointed Wiegert and fellow investigator Tom Fassbender in Dassey's direction, resulting in multiple interrogations that produced Dassey's eventual, convoluted confession.

But there were several problems with the state's confession evidence. First, much of it seemed implausible on its face. Second, when diving into the details, the story seemed even less plausible—even impossible. Third, a much bigger problem was that Dassey's tale was contradicted by all of the known physical evidence in the case. Fourth, the story was even self-contradictory in that it changed, on major points, from one minute to the next. And fifth, the biggest problem of all is that Dassey didn't actually provide the details that made up the confession; rather, his interrogators provided them and eventually convinced Dassey to agree.

How can this be? The answer, on some level, is simple: Wiegert and Fassbender interrogated Dassey using strategies, tactics, and tricks that were known (though perhaps not by them) to produce false confessions—particularly when used on young, learning-disabled, and highly compliant children.

The bulk of this book—parts II and III—will use plain English to expose and explain these tricks of the interrogation trade. It is important to keep in mind that these are, indeed, tricks of the trade. That is, Wiegert and Fassbender interrogated Dassey the way most police investigators are trained to interrogate their suspects. And what happened to Dassey happens to others—including many adults—on a regular basis in Wisconsin and throughout the country.

But before we start exploring interrogation tactics and false confessions, the next chapter discusses just how lucky Dassey is to have been able to mount a meaningful challenge to his conviction. If Halbach had disappeared just a few months earlier, and if everything else had played out as it did, Dassey would have had no shot whatsoever at winning his freedom.

2

FROM BLACK BOX TO GLASS HOUSE

Interrogations play a big role in many juvenile and adult criminal cases. In most parts of the country—particularly outside of the big cities, such as Milwaukee and Chicago in the Midwest—no case is too small for the police to pursue to the ends of the earth. And when the police don't have any evidence, they will often bring their target into the interrogation room to create that evidence.

For the first two years of my criminal defense practice, I primarily represented adult defendants charged with misdemeanors. And many of those cases involved confessions. But back in those days—the early 2000s in Kenosha, Wisconsin—interrogations were not recorded. And I quickly noticed a problem. First, the police reports said that my clients had admitted to the crimes with which they were now charged. But then, when I was able to meet with my clients, they would either deny having confessed or would admit to saying some things to the police that weren't true.

The clients' specific reasons for falsely confessing or quasi-confessing were as varied as the interrogators' tactics—more on those later. However, the clients' explanations all boiled down to this: inside that small, windowless interrogation room, the detective had somehow convinced them that if they just admitted some form of wrongdoing, they would be better off than if they maintained their innocence.

Sometimes the interrogators hinted that if the suspect confessed, he would be able to put it all behind him and leave the police station sooner. Other interrogators suggested that if the suspect confessed, the prosecutor would go easy on him down the road. "People who confess are always treated more fairly; but if you play hardball with me now, they'll play hardball with you later." (I soon learned that this assurance was false. When plea-bargaining on behalf of one of my earliest clients, I pointed out that, before I had been retained, the client was cooperative with the police and confessed. The prosecutor responded, "Well, that was stupid of him.")

Other interrogators had promised that if the suspect confessed, the judge would learn of his cooperation and things would go much more favorably for him in court. What they didn't say, of course, is that if the suspect simply remained silent, there often wouldn't be any "court" for him to go to. And sometimes, if interrogators had reason to believe the suspect was religious, they would even invoke God. "You don't want to lie when God is watching, do you?" (I never understood the appeal of that argument. Assuming the suspect bought into the premise, when would God *not* be watching?)

But regardless of the inducement, in each case the interrogator convinced the suspect that things would be much, much worse if he continued to deny guilt. After all, the interrogator would say, "What you did isn't that bad; it's lying about it afterwards that will get you into trouble. It's always better to be honest, and by denying this you are not being honest."

So what did the defense lawyer of the early 2000s do with this information from the client? First, the lawyer could file a motion arguing that the confession was not voluntary and, therefore, is not admissible at trial. Because many cases are built on little evidence other than the confession, a defense win at this stage means the prosecutor would be left with nothing and would dismiss the case. But here's how that motion hearing invariably played out.

On the one hand, the defendant would testify and try his best to explain to the judge why he confessed. For example, rather than confessing voluntarily, he did so because the interrogator promised to let him go home. (This inducement, of course, is usually a lie. Sometimes the suspect will be arrested despite the promise. Other times, the allegation is incredibly minor and the suspect is going to be released anyway, later to be served with a summons and complaint. But it is almost unimaginable that a suspect would be released *because* he confessed.)

On the other hand, the interrogator would testify and deny having made any such promises. This testimony would sound like the same broken record every time: "I just told the suspect, now the defendant, that 'I only want the truth.' And then he confessed."

Given these conflicting versions of events, which way do you think the court would rule? Would the elected trial judge shun the police detective and rule for a criminal? Or would the judge simply accept whatever came out of the detective's mouth? Even the Supreme Court of Wisconsin eventually conceded: "The result [was] often a credibility contest between law enforcement officials and the [accused], which law enforcement officials invariably win."[1]

Once the trial judge rubberstamped the defendant's confession as voluntary, and therefore admissible at trial, option number two for the criminal defense lawyer was to argue to the jury that the confession was not reliable—a legal distinction discussed later. In other words, the goal was to demonstrate for the jury that the confession was false and the defendant was innocent. Once again, it came down to a credibility battle.

On the one hand, the jury could side with the defendant. This is a person that typically has little education, no public speaking experience with which to persuade the jury, and a criminal record—something the jury usually hears about if the defendant testifies and sometimes even if he doesn't.[2]

On the other hand, jurors could side with the detective—a polished, trustworthy, semi-professional witness who had simply "invited" the defendant to the police station where he "questioned" him in an "interview room" and asked him merely to tell "the truth." (For obvious reasons, the detective would never admit that he "brought" the defendant to the police station where he "interrogated" him in an "interrogation room" until he "confessed in exchange for promises of leniency.")

Given these choices, which way do you think the jury would go?

Verdict: "We, the jury, find the defendant guilty."

The problem, of course, is that while nearly all confessions are persuasive to jurors, not all of them are true.

For the time period to which I am referring—again, the early 2000s—this is all we defense lawyers had to work with. The interrogation room was a black box. There was no tape recorder or camera—no way to see inside. We were left to fight a battle we were doomed to lose before it even began. The defense lawyer may as well have been stepping into the cage or ring with a professional fighter; the odds of winning were about the same.

Then, on July 7, 2005, just a few months before Halbach went missing, the law changed. In the case of *State v. Jerrell C.J.*, Jerrell challenged his confession in the court of appeals. Like Dassey, Jerrell was a teenager with a low IQ and bad grades who was interrogated without a parent or lawyer present. The interrogation went as follows:

At 9:10 a.m., Detective Span advised Jerrell of his Miranda rights. The detectives then began to question Jerrell. . . . Jerrell denied his involvement. The detectives challenged this denial and encouraged Jerrell to be "truthful and honest." . . . Jerrell again denied his involvement. The detectives again challenged this denial. . . . During the questioning, Jerrell was afforded food and bathroom breaks. . . . In the interrogation room, Detective Spano said Jerrell "started opening up about his involvement and everybody else's" somewhere between 1:00 and 1:30 p.m.[3]

Does any of that sound familiar? Substitute "Brendan" for "Jerrell," and the above paragraph could easily describe any one of Dassey's multiple interrogations. And much like the court in Dassey's case, this appeals court sided with the state. However, it issued a warning that was much stronger than many of its usual empty condemnations whenever police or prosecutors misbehave:

It is this court's opinion that it is time for Wisconsin to tackle the false confession issue. We need to take appropriate action *so that the youth of our state are protected from confessing to crimes they did not commit.* We need to find safeguards that will balance necessary police interrogation techniques to ferret out the guilty against the need to offer adequate constitutional protections to the innocent.[4]

The case was then accepted for review by the Supreme Court of Wisconsin—something it would later refuse to do in Dassey's case. There, Jerrell's lawyers asked the court to find that his confession was coerced, and also offered a solution for future cases: make the police record their interrogations. The lawyers argued that because it is "difficult to accurately recreate . . . months later in a courtroom what transpired in a lengthy interrogation," an "electronic recording would provide courts with the best evidence from which it [*sic*] can determine, under the totality of the circumstances, whether a juvenile's confession is voluntary."[5]

Not surprisingly, the government opposed such a rule, challenging the state supreme court's legal authority to implement the proposed reform and, further, arguing that the court should not intrude on how the police conduct their business.

In an unusually pro-defendant opinion, Wisconsin's high court rejected the prosecutor's arguments. "Plainly, this court has authority to adopt rules governing the admissibility of evidence."[6] And that's exactly what it did. "[W]e exercise our supervisory power to require that all custodial interrogation of juveniles in future cases be electronically recorded where feasible, and without exception when questioning occurs at a place of detention."[7] (More importantly for Jerrell, the court also reversed the appellate court and held that his confession was not voluntary, but rather was coerced, and therefore could not be used against him.)

Now that the police had to record their interrogations of juveniles, the interrogation room was turned from a black box into a glass house. Now we could see everything. With interrogations being recorded, judges would have "a more accurate and reliable record" and would be able to "conduct nuanced reviews to resolve admissibility issues."[8] There would be no more credibility battles where the outcome was decided before the witnesses even testified. Now, defense lawyers would be able to play the interrogation videos "to challenge misleading or false testimony" of the interrogators.[9]

Of course, as discussed in part IV of this book, state-level trial judges and appellate courts are not always willing to "conduct nuanced reviews" of interrogations. They are still eager to rubberstamp defendants' confessions, regardless of the interrogation methods used to extract them. Nonetheless, many positive things have come from recording police interrogations—something that Wisconsin now requires even for many adult suspects.[10]

Most notably, Dassey's lawyers would never have had a fighting chance if not for the numerous hours of recordings. Why? Because no interrogator would ever admit, and no judge would ever believe, what actually went on behind closed doors if it was not recorded. And this new window into the interrogation room also allows a previously impossible "show and tell." It was one thing for defense lawyers to try to describe what was happening inside the black box, but now we were able to expose these interrogation tactics with the full light of day. With this superior form of evidence—an audio or video recording instead of an after-the-fact reconstruction of events by the police detective—we are better able to answer two questions. Do suspects falsely confess? And if so, why?

3

"PEOPLE WHO ARE INNOCENT DON'T CONFESS"—DO THEY?

D o innocent people confess? Of course they do. We all know of real-life examples. False confessions in our part of the world date back several hundred years when women falsely confessed to being witches in Salem, Massachusetts.[1] A far more contemporary example is the Central Park jogger case, where the police interrogated five teenagers and got each one to falsely confess to a brutal rape.[2]

In the jogger case, there was no physical evidence against any of the five defendants; in fact, the DNA evidence recovered from the victim excluded all of them as suspects. Nonetheless, even with DNA in the defendants' favor, the prosecutor got five separate convictions. The only evidence the state had was the defendants' confessions, but that was enough. Fortunately, the boys (now men) were exonerated when the DNA sample was eventually matched to a specific person: the real rapist, who had no connection to the boys and admitted to acting alone when he attacked the victim.[3]

Unfortunately, this case is not an anomaly. Of the hundreds of wrongful convictions that have been overturned by DNA evidence, a large percentage—nearly one-third—involved false confessions.[4] This is not surprising. Research has shown that a defendant's confession is the most persuasive piece of evidence a jury will ever hear. Why? Because it is counterintuitive to most jurors that a person would confess to something he didn't do.[5] Therefore, jurors conclude, the confession must be true and the defendant must be guilty.

But these DNA exonerations are just the tip of the false-confession iceberg. The number of criminal convictions involving confession evidence is incredibly large; however, the number of those cases that involve DNA evidence is incredibly small. Most crimes to which suspects confess are things like burglary, theft, reckless behavior of some sort, sexual touching over the clothing, battery, and disorderly conduct—crimes that simply do not produce DNA evidence. How many of *these* defendants confessed falsely? We'll never know. Without DNA, they will rarely be able to prove their innocence; therefore, it is unlikely they will be able to prove that their confessions were false.

It is very easy to deny, or at least ignore, this entire line of false-confession evidence. For example, Dassey's prosecutor famously told the jury, "People who are innocent don't confess."[6] And if you're a prosecutor, such denial certainly makes it easier to sleep at night. But meanwhile, research psychologists are taking a close look at the phenomenon. Not only are they studying real-life false confessions, but they are also getting test participants—including some well-educated people—to falsely confess in controlled experiments.[7]

And this leads to our next question. Regardless of whether we're looking at a real-life criminal case or a controlled experiment in a laboratory, why would anyone confess to something he didn't do? The answer to this question is best explained with an analogy. Let's turn our attention to the single largest pool of false confessions in the world: the American plea-bargaining system.

Suppose you are charged with a crime. You are accused of criminally reckless behavior for the manner in which you drove your car. No one was hurt and no property was damaged. (Had there been actual harm to person or property, you would be facing a much wider array of criminal charges.) But because you allegedly drove this way with several people in the vicinity, you are charged with five counts of felony "second-degree recklessly endangering safety"[8]—one count for each person you supposedly placed in harm's way.[9] You are facing a maximum possible penalty of ten years in prison for each count,[10] which could be imposed consecutively,[11] thus exposing you to a possible penalty of fifty years. (Fortunately for you, even if you were convicted at trial on all counts, the actual sentence would probably be less than this theoretical, but legally permissible, maximum fifty-year term.)

You deny driving in the manner described in the criminal complaint. You are completely innocent of this alleged conduct. And from an evidentiary standpoint, the prosecutor has a weak case, and he knows it. So he immediately offers you the following deal: plead to one of the five felony counts, and he'll dismiss the other four and recommend one year of probation with no "conditional jail time" whatsoever.

You discuss this with your attorney, who tells you that pleading to a felony is serious business. Further, the sentence you will actually receive is up to the judge who might not go for probation. Your attorney also says that, for a plea deal to go through, you'd have to admit you are guilty—this judge, like many judges, will not accept a "no contest" plea. And an innocent person should not plead to a crime he did not commit, your attorney says.

You follow your attorney's advice and reject the plea offer. And as trial gets closer, the prosecutor fears having to try this garbage case—a case he could very well lose. Yet he still wants—in fact needs—a conviction for *something*. Dismissing the entire case at this point would be admitting that his office charges crimes it cannot prove, thus costing defendants and taxpayers a lot of money. So he makes you a new, much more attractive offer: plead to one negligence-based misdemeanor (not a felony) with a maximum possible sentence of only nine months in jail (not fifty years in prison). And for the actual sentence, he will recommend a $100 fine (not jail or even probation). To further sweeten the pot, he will recommend to the judge that, after a period of one year, your conviction should be expunged as long as you aren't convicted of any new crimes.

Wow! Your attorney was right. Rejecting that first offer was a great call. So you excitedly sit down to discuss this new offer. You are still completely innocent, but the calculus has now changed rather dramatically. The drawback to this new deal is that you'd still have to plead guilty to a crime, thus admitting guilt for something you didn't do. But on the plus side you will (1) save thousands of dollars in attorney's fees, (2) avoid numerous sleepless nights from intense anxiety before and during the multi-day trial, (3) reduce your maximum possible sentence by more than forty-nine years, (4) reduce your likely sentence from jail or probation to a mere $100 fine, and (5) create the very real chance that your misdemeanor crime will be expunged from your record in only one year.

You discuss this with your family, and it seems like a no-brainer: take the deal. But why would you falsely confess—by saying "I plead guilty" in open and public court—to something you didn't do? The answer is simple. After consulting with a criminal defense lawyer who was looking out for you, discussing the plea bargain with your family, and carefully weighing all of your options, you determined that admitting guilt to something you didn't do was *in your best interest.*

Maybe you made the right decision. Maybe the judge imposed the $100 fine (or a $250 fine to teach you a harsher lesson), sent you on your way, and even expunged your criminal record one year down the road. Or maybe it didn't work out the way you had hoped. Maybe the judge decided that a fine, in any amount, was too lenient for a person who put a human life in harm's way—after all, you did confess by pleading guilty to the reduced charge. So instead, maybe the judge gave you one year of probation, thirty days of conditional jail time, and a much stiffer $500 fine just for good measure. The point is that regardless of whether, in hindsight, your decision to admit guilt was a good one, you made that decision because, at the time, you believed it was in your best interest.

The same thing is true of admitting guilt in the interrogation room. Suspects do so because they believe, at that time, their decision to falsely confess is in their best interests. But how can that be? It's such a stupid decision! That's true: the decision to confess in the interrogation room is a stupid one—but it's not a surprising one.

Defendants who decide to plead guilty in court do so after consulting with their lawyers, talking the decision over with their families, and taking the time to think carefully about their options. The suspect in the interrogation room has no lawyer; instead, he is being "counseled" by police detectives who are trained to lie to him and convince him that he will be far better off if he confesses to them. And the detectives do this after isolating the suspect from family and friends and making sure he doesn't have the information, the support, or the time to rationally consider his true options.

As demonstrated above, the context of a false confession in court (in the form a guilty plea) is dramatically different from the context of a false confession in the interrogation room. It is not surprising, therefore, that when a defendant falsely confesses in court by pleading guilty he is sometimes making a bad decision; however, when a suspect falsely confesses in the interrogation room he is nearly always making a bad decision.

We saw in the above example how a defense attorney can convince a client—often correctly so—that falsely confessing in open and public court is in the client's best interest. But how did the interrogators convince Dassey that falsely confessing to them—without talking to an attorney for advice or discussing the decision with his family—was in *his* best interest?

That's what much of this book is about. It will expose and explain the numerous interrogation tactics that Wiegert and Fassbender used to convince an isolated, inexperienced, sixteen-year-old child to confess to the crimes of rape, murder, and mutilating a corpse. But before we explore these interrogation-room tactics, we'll first cover a few pre-interrogation tricks. With the right preparation and setup, the interrogators can win the battle before they even step onto the battlefield.

Part II
SETTING THE TABLE

4

DON'T LET FACTS GET IN THE WAY

In some cases, suspects have falsely confessed to crimes without any police prompting whatsoever. For example, John Mark Karr falsely confessed to murdering the child pageant queen JonBenet Ramsey. However, much like Dassey's story about Halbach, scientific testing disproved Karr's version of events: "The forty-one-year-old school teacher's DNA didn't match that found on the little girl's underwear."[1] But unlike Dassey's case, investigators examined the facts through an objective lens. Then, after comparing Karr's story to the actual evidence, "Colorado authorities said they weren't going to charge Karr with the murder."[2]

There are many possible explanations for this bizarre type of false confession. These include the confessor's "pathological need for attention" and the "blurring of fantasy and reality," which may cause the confessor to really believe that he committed the crime.[3] But spontaneous, unprompted false confessions, like Karr's, account for a small number of cases.

In the vast majority of false confession cases, the interrogator has formed a theory of the case and refuses to deviate from it. With this theory being immune to correction, the interrogator then forces it onto the suspect to obtain a statement that confirms the interrogator's predetermined beliefs. The interrogator's overconfidence, therefore, is one of the primary causes of the suspect's false confession. And this is the backdrop against which Mark Wiegert and Tom Fassbender's multiple interrogations of Dassey must be viewed.

Long before Wiegert and Fassbender deployed their tactics on Dassey, however, there were two other law enforcement agents that got hold of the learning-disabled teen. Shortly after Halbach's disappearance, but before her remains were found, investigating officers developed a theory of the case: Steven Avery had taken Halbach and was keeping her (or her corpse) on his property. And on November 6, 2005, Detectives O'Neill and Baldwin of the Marinette County Sheriff's Department interrogated

Dassey. Their goal was to obtain a statement that corroborated the state's theory. They wanted Dassey to confirm that Halbach was last seen *on* Avery's property *with* Avery.

O'Neill and Baldwin placed Dassey in the back of their unmarked squad car and aggressively interrogated him, without Miranda warnings. Dassey told them that, about a week earlier on Halloween, he got off his school bus, saw Halbach talking with Avery, and then walked up the road toward his home. O'Neill and Baldwin's interrogation went as follows:

Det. O'Neill: What happened to [Halbach]?

Dassey: She left.

Det. O'Neill: *She didn't leave.* What happened to that girl?

Dassey: Well she was, sh-she stayed there five minutes and then she left.

Det. O'Neill: Now that's what you're being told to say. . . . What happened to that girl?

Dassey: I don't know nothin', that's all I know. . . .

Det. O'Neill: Now is that what you saw or is that what you're being told to say?

Dassey: That's what I saw. She went out the driveway and then she turned left.[4]

Having Halbach driving away from Avery's property did not fit with the interrogators' version of events, so they got a bit more aggressive when forcing their theory of the case onto Dassey.

Det. Baldwin: Did she go into [Avery's] house, Brendan?

Dassey: No.

Det. Baldwin: Did she go into *your* house? Brendan?

Dassey: Huh?

Det. Baldwin: Did she go into *your* house?

Dassey: No.

Det. Baldwin: Where is she?

Dassey: I don't know.

Det. Baldwin: Brendan, you're not tellin' me something.

Dassey: She never came in my house.

Det. Baldwin: Okay, where is she? . . .

Dassey: I don't know anything.

Det. Baldwin: Well, why are you lying to me about this?

Dassey: I ain't.

Det. Baldwin: What do you mean you ain't? . . . Why is her vehicle on your land? . . . Whose fingerprints do you think we're gonna find in that van or in that truck of hers? . . . Your fingerprints gonna be in there? . . .

Det. O'Neill: [Halbach's] truck did not leave that place, it did not go out of the driveway and take a left.

Det. Baldwin: Brendan, what happened?

Dassey: I'm sayin' that's what happened.

Det. O'Neill: How soon after you got off the bus did [Halbach's] vehicle leave?

Dassey: Five minutes. It takes us like five minutes to walk down the road.

Det. O'Neill: So when you're walking down the road, is she leavin'?

Dassey: Yeah . . . *cuz we had to move on the side of the road so she could pass.*[5]

Dassey's statement was disastrous for the state. The state's theory was that Halbach never left Avery's property. But Dassey told O'Neill and Baldwin that not only did he witness Halbach leaving, but he even had to step to the side of the road so she could drive past him. This version of events strongly supported Avery's defense that he did not murder Halbach and, in fact, the last time he saw her she was driving away from him. This would mean that someone else must have killed her at a different location, put her body in her RAV4, and then drove it back to the Avery property. (This would also explain why Halbach's blood was found in the back of her own vehicle.)

Fortunately for the state, Wiegert and Fassbender eventually took over, and they have the superhuman ability to "know" what really happened. This is a special power that police interrogators believe they acquire through their training and experience—more on that later. So when Wiegert and Fassbender eventually interrogated Dassey, they were not searching for the truth; rather, they wanted to extract statements that corroborated "the truth" as they knew it. More specifically, "police interrogations . . . begin with the presumption of guilt. Interrogators then set out to confirm that presumption, using a variety of tactics in the process."[6] The problem, however, is that "[w]hile these tactics often extract true confessions from guilty suspects, they sometimes induce false confessions from innocent suspects."[7]

Wiegert and Fassbender believed that Dassey did, at some point, see Halbach on Avery's property. However, they were equally confident that Dassey did not see her drive away in her SUV. Rather, she remained on the property where Avery killed her and then burned her body right next to his trailer. And because they believed Dassey was lying, they interpreted every neutral or ambiguous fact in a way that confirmed, rather than contradicted, their theory of the case.

For example, Wiegert testified that the turning point came when he interviewed Dassey's younger relative, Kayla Avery. It was this interview that steered the investigation toward Dassey.

> Our purpose for going there was to interview Kayla in reference to Steve Avery. . . . And just about at the end of that interview, Kayla, uh, out of the blue, basically, came out and told us that, uh, she had a cousin by the name of Brendan, and that Brendan was, quote, acting up lately. So we asked Kayla what she meant by Brendan acting up lately. At that point Kayla told us that Brendan would just stare into space and start crying, basically, uncontrollably. She also told us that Brendan had—had lost approximately, what she estimated to be, about 40 pounds.[8]

There are reasons to be skeptical of Wiegert's testimony. For example, given that the interrogators were talking to Kayla about Avery and his alleged crime, why would she offer up irrelevant information, "out of the blue," about Dassey's weight? And would a girl her age even be aware enough to notice someone else's mood change or weight loss in the first place? If so, why would she describe crying and losing weight as "quote, acting up"? Those things sound more like signs that he had withdrawn, which is the opposite of "acting up." And what does Wiegert mean when *he* said *Kayla* said that Dassey would cry "basically" uncontrollably? Wiegert was obviously paraphrasing; what were Kayla's actual words? And did Wiegert ask an adult to confirm any of this information that Kayla spontaneously offered up "out of the blue"?

Of course, Wiegert and Fassbender did not want to confirm anything. They had the hook they needed. They already "knew" that Dassey was a liar—after all, Dassey's eyewitness account of Halbach driving away from the Avery property did not match their beliefs. And now, a young girl's unsubstantiated report about Dassey crying and losing weight was not only deemed reliable, but, in their minds, could only be explained this way: Dassey was experiencing gnawing guilt from witnessing, and perhaps even participating in, Halbach's murder.

It really is that simple. When a government agent is convinced that he knows something, he then interprets every piece of information in a way that substantiates his beliefs. Wiegert explained it to the jury like this: "So you take some of the things that [Dassey] told the Marinette officers [O'Neill and Baldwin] that just didn't seem to fit."[9] Wiegert continued, "And then his, uh, the losing weight, and the uncontrollable crying. Obviously, that, uh, points you in a direction you want to go."[10] Wiegert then testified that, after they set their sights on Dassey, "Uh, yes. Um, myself and Agent Fassbender had went to the Mishicot School System and, uh, that's where we met with Mr. Dassey that day."[11]

Wiegert had fooled himself into thinking he was Sherlock Holmes— picking up a subtle clue that only he could detect and then following it to discover the truth. But in reality, he was merely interpreting information to fit his preexisting beliefs. And if there is any doubt about Wiegert and Fassbender's confidence in their ability to divine the truth without the benefit of actual evidence, we needn't look further than their own words.

At the Mishicot High School interrogation, Fassbender told Dassey: "By your look I can tell you know of something, you saw something or somebody, somethin's laying heavy on ya. We wouldn't be here bothering you if we didn't know that."[12] And Wiegert was even clearer. "Tom [Fassbender] and I have been doing this job a long, long time, longer than you've been alive, and our experience and our knowledge in this job tells us that you're not being totally honest with us."[13]

Wiegert and Fassbender's confidence in their lie-detecting abilities is common among police interrogators; however, it is not justified.

The Reid School in Chicago claims to have developed a behavioral analysis protocol that allows trained investigators to detect deception at high levels of accuracy. Researchers, however, have demonstrated that investigators who use the Reid protocol are *no more accurate than untrained individuals* in detecting deception. Other researchers have shown that professionals who have been trained to detect deception in an interrogation context perform *no better than chance* at identifying deceptive persons. In short, it is unrealistic to think that police officers are, or can become, human lie detectors.[14]

But despite their (unwarranted) self-confidence, even Wiegert and Fassbender would have admitted that their ability to "know" Dassey was lying was only half the battle. Because their special brand of knowledge is not rooted in evidence, the suspect has to admit what the interrogators believe. Without the suspect's confession, the interrogators' beliefs are of little use in court. But getting the suspect to see the light isn't always easy. That's why the interrogation has to be carefully planned, starting with its location. As the next chapter explains, location is everything.

5

LOCATION, LOCATION, LOCATION

All of Dassey's police interrogators—O'Neill, Baldwin, Wiegert, and Fassbender—insisted that they were only after the truth. And when questioning Dassey, they wanted to know all kinds of details—including very mundane details—about things that happened weeks and even months earlier.

For example, O'Neill and Baldwin peppered Dassey with questions about the exact time he arrived home on October 31, 2005, whether he noticed Halbach standing near Avery when he got off his school bus, where he was standing when he claims Halbach drove past him and away from the property, what he had for dinner later that night, and what others in the Avery family may have seen or heard that day.

Similarly, Wiegert and Fassbender interrogated Dassey several times over a forty-eight-hour period, demanding details about what time Dassey saw his family members talking on the phone on October 31, what time he left his house to go to Avery's trailer, where Halbach's truck was parked when he last saw it, and, again, what others may have seen or heard that day.

Dassey complied with law enforcement's every request. And, according to Wiegert and Fassbender, Dassey's mother was also cooperative and gave them full access to her son. Wiegert even told Dassey before one of their interrogations, "I think we told you Brendan, we talked to mom, and mom is, is OK with this and good with this, and she just wants to talk to ya when we're, we're done."[1] He later added, "Your mom said be honest with us."[2]

So the question, then, is this: If you're an investigator collecting facts in your supposed search for the truth, where are you going to interview a shy, semiliterate, sixteen-year-old child with a "bad memory"?[3] Because both Dassey and his mother are being highly cooperative, you, the investigator, have your choice of the time and place for the interview.

Of course, you would want to interview Dassey at his home and with his mother present. The goal would be to make him as comfortable as possible so he can think clearly about the minutia you're interested in learning. And you'd also want to interview him at the place where the events unfolded. This way he could *show* you, for example, where Halbach's vehicle was parked when he saw it and where he was standing when she drove past him.

You would also want Dassey's mother close by, not only to make him more comfortable, but also to provide information that Dassey might not be able to recall—for example, what she made for dinner on a particular night. And interviewing Dassey at his home would provide additional benefits, such as being near things that may refresh his memory and even provide more reliable answers than he could. For example, with regard to what time Dassey saw his family members talking on the phone on Halloween, what could be better evidence than the phone bill to pin down the precise time of the calls? And where is that phone bill most likely to be located? That's right: at Dassey's home. And who is most likely to know where to find it? Right again: Dassey's mother.

But none of Dassey's interrogators really wanted to talk to him for the purpose of learning anything. As the last chapter explained, interrogations are a guilt-presumptive process. By the time O'Neill, Baldwin, Wiegert, and Fassbender got hold of Dassey, they already believed they knew what happened, and they were only interested in getting Dassey to say things that confirmed their preexisting theory.

And it appears that, contrary to Ken Kratz's claim, Dassey *was* a suspect from the very first interrogation by O'Neill and Baldwin a week after Halbach went missing. As the last chapter demonstrated, the interrogators repeatedly accused Dassey of lying, pressured him to change his story, and even grilled him as to whether the then-missing (and possibly dead) Halbach might be found inside *his* house. And to remove any remaining doubt about how they viewed Dassey, Baldwin pressed, "Is that girl alive, Brendan? Yeah, you do know, Brendan. *Were you involved in this?*"[4]

Similarly, in Wiegert and Fassbender's first "interview" of Dassey—an interrogation without Miranda warnings conducted under the pretense that Dassey was merely a "witness" and was free to leave—Wiegert grilled the child: "Did you have anything to do with the death of Teresa

Halbach?"[5] That question is not commonly asked of a witness; rather, it is a question for a suspect.

But because Dassey's interrogators were not interested in learning information, they did not question him at his home or in the presence of his mother. Given their real objectives, they did not want Dassey to be comfortable; rather, they wanted to isolate him and make him as uncomfortable as possible.

> Police investigators typically isolate suspects from family and friends before an interrogation begins. . . . Social isolation within unfamiliar surroundings leads to anxiety and a desire to remove one's self from an uncomfortable situation. In this kind of situation, individuals often comply, to a surprisingly high degree, with their interrogators' demands.[6]

Isolating suspects and putting them in unfamiliar surroundings is by far the most commonly used police interrogation tactic.[7] And, as expected, it worked brilliantly on Dassey. To say that Dassey felt "anxiety" due to his isolation while being interrogated is probably an understatement.

For example, on November 6, 2005, O'Neill and Baldwin stopped the car in which Dassey was a passenger. They seized and impounded the car, leaving Dassey dependent on them for a ride home. They then put Dassey in the back of their squad to interrogate him.[8] They knew Dassey was scared straight, and this is exactly what they wanted. When they repeatedly pressured him to adopt their version of events—that Dassey did *not* see Halbach drive away from what they believed to be the scene of her murder—O'Neill even said, "let's get beyond being *scared*; let's get beyond the idea of you gettin' in trouble and *goin' to jail*. . . . Did you actually see her leave or did she stay there?"[9]

Similarly, Wiegert and Fassbender isolated Dassey by taking him out of class and interrogating him in a room at Mishicot High School, again in a room at the Two Rivers Police Department, and then again in a room at the Manitowoc County Sheriff's Department. The setting for this last interrogation, which was very much like the setting for his earlier interrogations, was as follows:

> On March 1, officers initiated contact with Brendan by pulling him out of his high school class and driving him to the Manitowoc Police [*sic*] Department, where he was marooned alone. . . . He was questioned

behind a closed door in a small room, with his questioners seated such that they blocked Brendan's path to exit. If Brendan had tried to leave, he would have been stopped. . . . Brendan was not told that he was free to leave on March 1. Instead, he was subjected to a police-dominated interrogation that included deception, long police monologues, leading questions, suggestions of leniency, and rejections of his claims of innocence.[10]

All of Dassey's interrogators easily got the mentally challenged child where they wanted him: isolated from family, removed from familiar surroundings, and put into highly uncomfortable situations where authority figures scared the living daylights out of him. They also made clear that, in order to relieve the pressure they had placed on him, he had to adopt their version of events.

But before the interrogators could get to the meat of the matter—the interrogation—they had one more hurdle: Dassey's Miranda rights. As the following chapters explain, just as the interrogators carefully planned the location for their questioning, so too did they plan ways to prevent Dassey from invoking his right to remain silent and his right to an attorney.

6

MIRANDA TO THE RESCUE?

Once interrogators isolate a suspect on the government's home field, they have several tactics designed to ramp up the pressure. For example, consider the interrogation at Mishicot High School. After Wiegert and Fassbender got Dassey alone, they falsely assured him that "we're not here ta, ta jump in your face or get into ya or anything like that."[1] But as soon as those words spilled out of their mouths, they made a 180-degree turn:

> We've got people back at the . . . district attorney's office, and they're lookin' at this now saying there's no way that Brendan Dassey was out there and didn't see something. They're talking about trying to link Brendan Dassey with this event. . . . They're saying that Brendan had something to do with it or the cover up of it which would mean Brendan Dassey would *potentially be facing charges* for that.[2]

After this scare tactic, they offered a reprieve. "We said no, let us talk to him, give him the opportunity to come forward with the information that he has, and get it off his chest."[3] They then pressed Dassey for details: "you built the fire, and we believe that's, that's where Teresa was cooked."[4] They continued, "I'm afraid you saw something. . . . Did you see a hand, a foot, something in that fire? Her bones? Did you smell something that was not too right?"[5]

This must have been an overwhelming shock to Dassey's system. One minute, the unsuspecting child is sitting in class learning mundane facts about history or science or prepositional phrases or whatever; the next minute, two government agents are grilling him about cooked human body parts and telling him that, unless he comes forward with the scoop, the prosecutor will charge *him* for the crimes. How Dassey refrained from vomiting and passing out on the spot remains a mystery.

But the law, at least in theory, is supposed to protect people in Dassey's predicament. The overwhelming pressure that Wiegert and Fassbender were putting on him is exactly the type of situation for which the now famous, constitutionally required Miranda warning was intended. "That is, the goal of the Miranda warning was to ensure that suspects are fully informed of several important rights—including the right to remain silent and the right to an attorney—*before succumbing to police pressures and agreeing to speak.*"[6]

Thanks largely to police-themed television dramas, most readers would be able to recite at least some parts of the Miranda warning. Oddly, however, there is no specific language required to satisfy the mandates set forth by the Supreme Court in *Miranda v. Arizona*.[7] In fact, hundreds of different versions of the warning are in use throughout the United States.[8] Even within a particular state, such as Wisconsin, the warning will vary among law enforcement agencies. Nonetheless, a typical Miranda warning—to the extent such a creature exists—goes something like this:

> (1) You have the right to remain silent; (2) Anything you say can and will be used against you in a court of law; (3) You have the right to consult with a lawyer before questioning and to have a lawyer present with you during questioning; (4) If you cannot afford to hire a lawyer, one will be appointed to represent you at public expense before or during any questioning, if you so wish; and (5) If you decide to answer questions now without a lawyer present, you have the right to stop the questioning and remain silent at any time you wish, and the right to ask for and have a lawyer at any time you wish, including during the questioning.[9]

In theory, this language appears to protect suspects from pressure-cooker situations like the one Dassey found himself in with Wiegert and Fassbender. However, a very curious thing about Miranda is the way the warning is delivered: *the police* are the ones who must convey the warning to the suspect. But, despite what Deputy Friendly taught us in grade school, there are many times when the police are not our friends. And one of those times is when they sit down to question us in a criminal investigation. Despite the interrogators' false assurances that they are there to help the suspect and give him the "opportunity" to help himself, the police and the suspect are not on the same side. Rather, the interests of the police are at direct and irreconcilable odds with the interests of the suspect.[10]

Wiegert and Fassbender's interrogation of Dassey is an excellent illustration of this conflict of interest. If Dassey had acted in his best interest and invoked one of his Miranda rights, Wiegert and Fassbender would have been far worse off. If Dassey had decided to remain silent or at least consult with a lawyer—most of whom, in turn, would have told him to remain silent—the government would have had a weaker case against Avery and no case whatsoever against Dassey. On the other hand, by getting Dassey to talk, Wiegert and Fassbender dramatically strengthened the state's case against Avery and even created an entirely new case by making a murderer out of Dassey as well.

The point is this: the police want, and often need, the suspect to talk. Without the suspect's statement, the government will have a weak case or no case. Yet it is the police who are supposed to warn the suspect about the dangers of talking. In theory, this is a conflict of interest. In practice, however, it poses no problem at all.[11] The reason is that, whenever the Constitution conveys a right or a protection like the Miranda warning, the police—with the help of prosecutors and judges—simply develop ways to get around it.

Unlike the popular television dramas where the police read the suspect his Miranda rights clearly, loudly, and proudly—almost as if it were a government victory speech—the real-life police don't want to do that and have developed several tactics to flat-out decimate Miranda's safeguards. And Wiegert and Fassbender used one of those tactics when they interrogated Dassey at Mishicot High School on February 27, 2006. As the next chapter explains, they simply (and legally) skipped Dassey's Miranda warning entirely and instead went straight to the questioning.

BYPASSING MIRANDA

When the police try to talk to a suspect, they do so because they want the suspect to, well, *talk*. The police therefore do not want to read the suspect the Miranda warning because, if they do, the suspect might invoke those rights and refuse to talk. Fortunately for the police, the law requires them to read the Miranda warning only if both of the following are true: first, the suspect is in police custody; and second, the police are questioning, or interrogating, the suspect.[1] Thus, to bypass Miranda entirely and avoid reading a suspect his rights, the police simply need to structure the police-suspect interaction so that one of those two things is *not* true.

For example, assume that a suspect is in custody, and the police would like him to make a statement. Instead of reading him his Miranda rights, hoping he waives those rights, and then asking him questions, the police can simply get the suspect talking in other ways. If the police can get statements without technically asking the suspect any questions, then no Miranda warnings are needed. This tactic is nicely illustrated in the case of *McClellan v. State*,[2] which I discussed in a recent law review article:

> All parties agreed that the defendant was in custody at the time of [his] statement; the issue was whether he was being . . . questioned. While sitting with the arrested defendant, a detective decided to engage him "in general shop talk about"—what else?—"worthless checks and forgeries," the very crimes with which the defendant was being charged. During the course of this "shop talk," the detective called the defendant "an amateur," and further questioned him about his alleged crimes, including asking, "[H]ow did you do it?"[3]

The defendant, unaware of his Miranda rights, reportedly answered the detective's questions about the alleged crimes, including telling him how he committed them. But when the defense lawyer later moved to suppress the defendant's statements because the police never read him his rights, the government was able to defeat the motion by arguing that the detective's "shop talk" was not the same thing as asking the defendant questions. And because the police only engaged in "shop talk," rather than direct questioning, the defendant was not entitled to a Miranda warning. And because the police did not violate Miranda, the prosecutor was allowed to use the defendant's statements against him at trial.[4]

In reality, of course, the so-called "shop talk" *was* direct questioning. The words "How did you do it?" constitute a question, no matter which way or how many ways you slice it. Yet by merely putting a different label on it, the police, prosecutor, and judge were able to accomplish their shared goal: get the defendant's statement into evidence at trial and get a conviction.

It really is that easy—in most cases. But that tactic probably would not have worked on Dassey—a shy, quiet, and withdrawn child who was not likely to take the bait and freely partake in "shop talk" with Wiegert and Fassbender. Rather, as the footage in *Making a Murderer* demonstrated, the interrogators had to drag the words out of him by alternating a variety of threats and promises, asking repeated and leading questions, touching him, and employing several other interrogation tactics. Therefore, because Wiegert and Fassbender would not be able to later claim they were merely engaging in "shop talk" rather than asking direct questions, they had to employ a different tactic: question Dassey while he was technically not in custody. No custody, no Miranda.

How did Wiegert and Fassbender accomplish this? Just like the interrogator in *McClellan*, they resorted to a superficial, form-over-substance trick. When they took Dassey out of his classroom on February 27, 2006, they did not put him in the squad car and drive him to the police station for questioning. Instead, they took him to a room at Mishicot High School and questioned him there.

Once they were alone with Dassey, they did two things. First, to avoid any future defense-lawyer argument that Dassey was not free to leave—and, therefore, was in custody and was entitled to a reading of the Miranda warning—they told Dassey that "you're not under arrest, you know that."[5] And second, to ensure that Dassey would cooperate with them instead of clamming up or even walking out of the room, the interrogators immediately made clear what they wanted. "I would really appreciate if you would just kinda relax and open up with us. . . . I want you to talk to us, talk about what you're thinking about, feeling maybe."[6] From there, they were off to the races.

This was a low-risk strategy for Wiegert and Fassbender to employ. They knew it was safe to tell Dassey he was not in custody, as there was no way Dassey was going to defy two adult authority figures who had just removed him from class for the purpose of talking to him. They knew there was virtually zero chance Dassey was going to stand up and walk out of the room in response to their direct questions. Therefore, isolating him for an in-school interrogation was the functional equivalent of an in-custody interrogation, but without Dassey technically being "in custody" for purposes of Miranda.

Given that Wiegert and Fassbender structured Dassey's interrogation as out-of-custody questioning, they were able to skip the Miranda warning and launch straight into the heart of the matter: "I'm afraid you saw something. . . . Did you see a hand, a foot, something in that fire? Her bones?"[7] And they would not take "no" for an answer: "You're not being totally honest with us. . . . I find it quite difficult to believe . . . that you wouldn't have seen something like a hand, or a foot, a head, hair, something. OK. We know you saw something."[8] And when Dassey finally took the bait and agreed with some of their statements, they rewarded him while prodding him for more: "You're startin' to, you're starting to get it out now OK. It'll be all right . . . get it all out, it doesn't do any good to get half of it out."[9]

As discussed earlier, Wiegert and Fassbender had to interrogate Dassey several times before they could "get it all out." And some of those interrogations did take place in a police station. In fact, later on February 27, they questioned Dassey at the Two Rivers Police Department for the second leg of their four-part, two-day interrogation tour. Due to the location of that questioning, it was much more likely to be considered an in-custody interrogation. Therefore, Wiegert and Fassbender did read Dassey his Miranda rights. But as the next chapter explains, when the police can't bypass Miranda entirely, and instead must read the suspect a standard Miranda warning, they have developed numerous techniques to induce the suspect to waive, rather than invoke, those important rights.

8

OVERCOMING MIRANDA

Before their *in*-custody interrogations, Wiegert and Fassbender read Dassey his Miranda rights, including his right to remain silent and his right to a free-of-charge lawyer to advise him before and during questioning. Yet both times Dassey waived his rights and talked. But why, after hearing the Miranda warnings—including the warning that anything he said could be used against him—would Dassey agree to waive his rights and talk even once, let alone multiple times?

First, Dassey is not alone in waiving his rights. Several large-scale studies show that approximately 80 percent of real-life criminal suspects waive their rights and talk to the police.[1] And in 2012, Anthony Domanico, Lawrence T. White, and I published a study-turned-article discussing a sample of twenty-nine police interrogations in Wisconsin in which twenty-seven, or 93 percent, of the suspects waived their rights.[2] (Based on this sample, Wisconsin interrogators are better than the national average at getting suspects to talk.) One reason for this high rate is that suspects typically do not understand the Miranda warning and the important rights they are giving up when they decide to answer their interrogators' questions.

For example, the Wisconsin Miranda warning we tested—which was reproduced in chapter 6 and is very similar to the warnings that Wiegert and Fassbender read to Dassey—requires a tenth-grade reading level in order to comprehend 75 percent of its meaning.[3] Yet, most suspects, including Dassey, read at a much lower level. Given Dassey's limited reading abilities and low general intelligence, he likely understood very little about the substance and importance of his Miranda rights.

Second, chapter 6 also explained that the police have a conflict of interest in the Miranda process: they are legally required to tell the suspect about the dangers of talking, but they don't want to convey that message too clearly or the suspect might actually refuse to speak to them. Therefore, when reading Miranda, the police will minimize its importance, thus inducing the suspect to waive, rather than invoke, the underlying rights. In our study of Wisconsin interrogations, nearly half of the interrogators used minimization tactics that "ranged from saying the procedure is just *'something we have to do,'* to presenting Miranda as a mere formality—the appetizer before the main course, so to speak."[4]

Dassey's interrogators were no different. Before reading Dassey his Miranda warning at the Two Rivers Police Department, Wiegert said, "But before we ask any questions Brendan, um, I have to read you your rights. It's *just what we have to do*—steps OK."[5] Such minimization, combined with Dassey's inability to comprehend the substance of the warning, was probably enough to induce him to waive his rights. But just in case it wasn't, Wiegert and Fassbender employed other waiver-inducing strategies.

Third, speed matters. It is commonly known that "as speakers speak faster and faster, listeners comprehend less and less."[6] And in our study of real-life Wisconsin interrogations, the police "spoke significantly faster—*31 percent faster*—during the Miranda procedure" than before and after reading the Miranda warning.[7] In fact, in the twenty-nine real-life interrogations we studied, the interrogators delivered the Miranda warning at an average speed of 268 words per minute.[8] This makes an already difficult-to-understand warning nearly impossible for most suspects to comprehend. And when a suspect doesn't grasp the substance and significance of his rights, he is more likely to waive them.

But what about Wiegert and Fassbender? In addition to minimizing the importance of Miranda, they also read the warning very quickly, thus decreasing Dassey's comprehension and increasing the odds he would waive, rather than invoke, his rights. When delivering the Miranda warning before the fateful interrogation at the Manitowoc County Sheriff's Department, Wiegert spoke at more than 270 words per minute,[9] leaving Dassey with little hope of understanding even the importance, let alone the substance, of the language that Wiegert was rattling off.

Fourth, timing is everything. Chapter 7 explained how Wiegert and Fassbender interrogated Dassey at length, without Miranda warnings, at Mishicot High School on February 27, 2006. Later, Dassey likely viewed the Mirandized questioning at the Two Rivers Police Department—questioning by the same interrogators, on the same day, regarding the same topic—as a mere continuation of the earlier questioning. In essence, although they did read Dassey his Miranda rights, they did so well into the long, multipart interrogation. By that time, the horse had already left the barn, and the warnings lost what little meaning they might have otherwise had for Dassey.

And with regard to the interrogation at the Manitowoc County Sheriff's Department, the interrogators' timing of their Miranda reading was impeccable. Wiegert and Fassbender first told Dassey to come to the police station so they could continue their questioning that began less than forty-eight hours earlier. Then, after he agreed, they read him his Miranda rights, which concluded as follows: "Understanding those rights, do you want to talk with us?"[10]

Of course, the answer was "yes," as Dassey had already agreed to do so and, in fact, was in the back of a moving police vehicle en route to the sheriff's department when they read him his rights and asked that question. Given the interrogators' strategic timing, there was simply no chance the highly compliant child would demand that they stop the police vehicle so he could invoke a set of rights he never understood in the first place.

But assume, for a moment, that Dassey was able to read at a high enough level to understand the substance of the Miranda warning. Further, pretend that Wiegert did not minimize the importance of Dassey's rights and, additionally, did not race through the warnings at the breakneck speed of more than 270 words per minute. Finally, pretend that Wiegert actually read Dassey his rights at the very beginning, rather than somewhere in the middle, of the four-part, two-day interrogation. Even assuming away all of these problems, would Dassey—or even a hypothetical, intelligent, well-informed, adult suspect—know what rights he would be giving up if he agreed to speak? In other words, did the Miranda warning itself make any sense?

On February 27, before the interrogation at the Two Rivers Police Department, Wiegert awkwardly delivered a Miranda warning that read, in part, as follows:

> You have the right to, you have the right to talk, to a lawyer for advice *before* we ask you any questions and have him with you *during* questioning. You have this right to the advice and presence of a lawyer even though you cannot afford to hire one. *We have no way of getting you a lawyer* but one will be appointed for you if you wish and if and when *you go to court.*[11]

This cop-speak raises several questions. First, as the law requires, Wiegert tells Dassey that he has the right to consult with a lawyer "before we ask you any questions" and "during questioning." But then, in classic cop fashion, he reverses course: "we have no way of getting you a lawyer."

Is this even a proper Miranda warning given that it contradicts itself? Worse yet, it actually says the opposite of what the law requires by telling the suspect he will *not* be provided with a lawyer "before" or "during questioning." Alternatively, if the police "have no way of getting" the suspect a lawyer "before" or "during questioning," does the suspect really have that right to begin with? After hearing this garbled mess of a Miranda warning, a reasonable suspect in Dassey's position may wonder: What, exactly, *are* my rights that the police are asking me to give up?

Second, Wiegert then tells Dassey that a lawyer would not be provided until "you go to court." Go to court for what? Up until this point, the interrogators had been lying to Dassey, telling him that if he told them what they wanted to hear (which he did) they would protect him from a criminal prosecution. So does that mean Dassey would get a lawyer if he goes to court to testify in Steven Avery's case? Given all of the police deception, what other "court" could Dassey possibly have been imagining at that point?

Third, Wiegert's Miranda warning left open an even bigger question. It clearly warned Dassey that "anything you say can be used against you."[12] But what about what Dassey does *not* say? In other words, if Dassey elects to remain silent, could his silence be used against him as evidence of his guilt? The answer is "no"; as a general rule, *post*-Miranda silence is not admissible at trial. Nonetheless, many suspects think that if they remain silent—or worse yet, lawyer-up—they will look guilty to a jury.[13] And the Miranda warning does nothing to dispel this misconception, which is yet another reason that suspects are inclined to waive their rights and talk to the police.

Fourth and finally, even if Wiegert had read Dassey an intelligible Miranda warning, Dassey probably still would have waived, rather than invoked, his rights. The reason is that Wiegert did not give him an actual choice in the matter. Instead, he presented the highly compliant child with only one option: waive the rights. More specifically, on February 27, Wiegert read Dassey his Miranda rights from a form that concluded as follows: "I understand what my rights are, I am willing to answer questions and to make statements. I do not want a lawyer. I understand and know what I am doing."[14]

Nowhere on the form was Dassey provided with an alternative such as this: "I *don't* understand my rights, particularly because you first told me that I have the right to a lawyer before and during questioning, but then you told me that you have no way of getting me a lawyer." Similarly, nowhere on the form was Dassey given this option: "I am *not* willing to answer questions or to make a statement." And, of course, nowhere on the form was Dassey allowed to choose this alternative: "I *don't* understand or know what I am doing because I am a child being railroaded by two cops who told me they were acting as my father figure and not as government agents." (How to reform the Miranda warning to give a suspect some actual choices is the subject of chapter 32.)

Dassey therefore reluctantly accepted the one option with which he was presented, "to answer questions and to make statements":

Wiegert: Do you agree with that?

Brendan: Yeah.

Wiegert: You have to speak up a little bit.

Brendan: Yeah.

Wiegert: Yes?

Brendan: Yes.[15]

The hard part was now behind Wiegert and Fassbender; however, there was still one more Miranda-related issue for them to worry about. The warning they had read to Dassey, like the warning discussed in chapter 6, informed him of the following right: "You also have the right to *stop answering questions at any time* until you talk to a lawyer."[16] Arguably, this was another illusory right given that seconds earlier Wiegert also told him, "We have no way of getting you a lawyer."[17] Nonetheless, it was theoretically possible, though highly unlikely, that Dassey might remember his right to "stop answering questions at any time" and bring the interrogation to a grinding halt. Therefore, as the next chapter explains, Wiegert and Fassbender pulled one more Miranda-related ploy out of their sizable bag of tricks.

9

NEGATING MIRANDA

In theory, Dassey could have clammed up in the middle of the interrogation and invoked his constitutional right to stop answering questions. But in reality, suspects rarely do so. While "eighty percent [of suspects] waive their rights . . . the more troubling statistic is this: out of those eighty percent who do agree to talk, virtually none subsequently assert their rights during the interrogation."[1]

Dassey fell into this camp. He kept talking—or, more accurately, he kept agreeing with his interrogators' statements—which earned him a cell in the juvenile detention facility and, ultimately, in a Wisconsin state prison. But why didn't Dassey, and virtually every other suspect who initially agreed to talk to the police, simply stop answering questions when things got too intense? When Wiegert and Fassbender kept pressing Dassey to admit guilt, why didn't he simply say, "I want to stop the questioning and talk to a lawyer"?

There are several reasons why Dassey didn't invoke this mid-interrogation right. By the time he realized he was in hot water, Wiegert and Fassbender were well into the interrogation. Dassey, therefore, had probably long forgotten his Miranda rights. Even more likely, as explained in chapter 8, he probably never understood them to begin with. And this fifth prong of the Miranda warning is particularly difficult to understand—even for suspects who are literate adults. In the previously discussed study of twenty-nine real-life Wisconsin interrogations, this fifth prong had a "Flesch-Kincaid readability grade level of . . . 18.7."[2] In other words, "The fifth prong—regarding the right to stop answering questions after the right to silence is initially waived—is worded in such a way that even college-educated suspects may not fully understand their rights."[3]

To make matters worse, this portion of *Wiegert's* Miranda warning was even more difficult to comprehend. In fact, it defied comprehension;

it was self-contradictory and nonsensical. Here, again, is the relevant portion from the February 27, 2006, Miranda warning:

> You have the right to, you have the right to talk, to a lawyer for advice before we ask you any questions and have him with you during questioning. . . . We have no way of getting you a lawyer. . . . If you wish to answer questions now without a lawyer present, you have the right . . . to stop answering questions at any time until you talk to a lawyer.[4]

So is Wiegert telling Dassey that he has the right to "stop answering questions" until he can "talk to [the] lawyer" that Wiegert has "no way of getting" him?

Wiegert and Fassbender knew there was only an infinitesimally small chance that the highly compliant, learning-disabled child would somehow remember the words "stop answering questions" and, on top of that, muster the courage to affirmatively invoke that right mid-interrogation. Nonetheless, they didn't want to take any chances. So right after the initial Miranda waiver (and again several times throughout the interrogation) they employed yet another Miranda-related trick: they simply negated the warnings they had just read to Dassey.

The Miranda warning, despite all of its faults, does make clear that the interrogators are working for the government and are not acting on behalf of the suspect. If this warning has any effect at all, it would make the suspect less likely to talk. Wiegert and Fassbender therefore quickly negated it by repeatedly saying the opposite to Dassey. Rather than accurately representing themselves as government agents, they frequently expressed concern for their target and routinely called him their "buddy."[5] Far more troubling, they assured Dassey they were acting not as cops but as his father figure.[6] And they continually lied by promising, over and over, that they would stand by him, were on his side, and were in his corner.

> Like I said, Mark and I are not going to leave you high and dry. I got a very, very important appointment at 3:00 today. Well I ain't leavin' for the appointment until I'm sure you're taken care of . . . so go ahead and talk to us about what you saw in the fire.[7]

By constantly reminding Dassey that they were there to help him, Wiegert and Fassbender completely negated Miranda's warning that they were, in fact, his adversaries. They left no room for doubt in Dassey's mind. Their repeated lies left him believing that they were on *his* side.

Similarly, despite its many flaws, another thing Miranda effectively does is to warn suspects that anything they say can be used against them. Wiegert and Fassbender quickly negated this warning by, once again, telling Dassey the exact opposite. They started by telling him that his statements would *not* be used against him. They explained that they understood why he didn't want to talk: "you were scared . . . that you would be implicated in this" and "that you might get arrested and stuff like that."[8] However, they assured him, "from what I'm seeing . . . I'm thinking you're all right."[9] "Ok, you don't have to worry about things."[10] More to the point, *"you have nothing to worry about."*[11]

Then, to make their 180-degree turnabout complete, they also told Dassey that his statements would actually be used *for* him: "We wanna go back and tell people that, you know, Brendan told us what he knew. We wanna be able to tell people that Brendan was honest, he's not like Steve, he's honest, he's a good guy."[12] To remove any doubt about the benefits that would inure from talking, they spelled it out for Dassey: "And by you talking with us, it's, *it's helping you.* OK?"[13] They even got incredibly specific with their lies. "Brendan, I'm going to ask you a difficult question, OK? Did you help [Avery] put that body in the fire? *If you did it's OK."*[14]

By telling Dassey they were not his adversaries but rather his friends, and by telling him his statements would not be used against him but rather to help him, Wiegert and Fassbender completely negated any impact the Miranda warning might have otherwise had on the child. This ensured that he would not invoke his rights, mid-interrogation, after he initially waived them.

But let's, for a moment, imagine the highly improbable. What if Dassey *had* tried to stop answering questions after he had started talking? Would Wiegert and Fassbender have honored his request? Probably not. To conclude our discussion of Miranda-related topics, we must leave Dassey's case and look at another Wisconsin case where a defendant attempted to stop the questioning and invoke his mid-interrogation right to remain silent. The defendant told his interrogators in no uncertain terms: "You ain't listening to what I'm telling you. You don't want to hear what I'm saying. You want me to admit to something I didn't do and *I got nothin[g] more to say to you. I'm done. This is over."*[15]

Was this crystal-clear invocation of the mid-interrogation right to stop answering questions enough to actually stop the interrogation? Not by a long shot. The problem with the defendant's request, the Wisconsin court believed, is that while it *might* have been construed as an attempt to invoke the right to remain silent, "it was [also] reasonable for the detectives to conclude that his statement was merely a fencing mechanism to get a better deal."[16]

This is an odd conclusion given that prosecutors, not the police, cut plea deals. But it's just another example of how the police, prosecutors, and judges conspire to take plain language and twist it into whatever form will benefit the state. Given this, the odds that Dassey—a shy, highly compliant, mentally challenged child—could have successfully invoked his right to remain silent are about the same as Wiegert and Fassbender making it through an interrogation without lying to their suspect.

10

GETTING TO KNOW ALL ABOUT YOU

Wiegert and Fassbender had put in a lot of thought and effort up to this point. One thing they had worked very hard to do was to convince Dassey they were his friends and were there to help. Among numerous other examples, Fassbender said, "I'm your friend right now, but I . . . gotta believe in you and if I don't believe in you, I can't go to bat for you."[1]

This tactic actually served a dual purpose. It not only eliminated the risk that Dassey would invoke his right to remain silent mid-interrogation, but it also helped jump-start the substantive conversation. If Dassey believed that talking to his new "friend" was to his benefit, because his "friend" would "go to bat" for him, then Dassey would be more likely to, well, *talk*. And toward this same end, there was one more thing the interrogators wanted to do before unleashing their arsenal of interrogation tactics: build a rapport with Dassey.

Rapport building is simply commonsense; it's something we do in many different contexts. For example, if a person is interested in dating someone who is, essentially, a stranger, he or she does not simply walk up to that stranger and ask for a date. Rather, he or she will dramatically increase the odds of success by first attempting to build a rapport. "Hello." "How are you doing today?" "Where do you work?" "That's a great jacket you're wearing." "Oh, you know John Jones? How is he doing?" And the same thing is true of interrogators. They don't just sit a suspect down and start asking questions. An interrogator knows that the amount and quality of information he will be able to extract from the suspect is positively correlated with the level of rapport he is first able to establish.

More specifically, interrogators "may use *pre*-Miranda conversation to build rapport, which is important to obtaining a Miranda waiver."[2] Similarly, interrogators also use rapport building *post*-Miranda to get the suspect comfortable and talking more freely. That is, rapport building often occurs "after the suspect waived his Miranda rights," and is therefore "directed at eliciting a subsequent confession, rather than an initial Miranda waiver."[3]

The more astute among us can see through attempts at rapport building—whether they are coming from a would-be date or a government agent. Even so, many otherwise intelligent defendants have told me how surprised they were upon first learning they had been criminally charged. Their reason: the detective who questioned them "seemed like such a nice guy." In any case, the quiet and withdrawn Brendan Dassey most certainly was not sophisticated enough to recognize Wiegert and Fassbender's rapport-building tactics, which started with feigned interest in Dassey's well-being and emotional state.

Fassbender kicked off one of their interrogations by asking, "So how ya doin' Brendan since, ah, the last time we talked to you?"[4] Wiegert also chimed in. "All right. How you doin' buddy?"[5] To really build trust, the interrogators would slip into psychologist mode. "We're here more ta maybe let you talk . . . about how you've been feeling lately and stuff. . . . Go ahead and tell us what's been bothering ya."[6] And, as we saw in earlier chapters, playing the father figure doesn't hurt either: "I'm a father that has a kid your age too. I wanna be here for you."[7]

Other ways they built rapport was to show an interest in Dassey's family and friends. For example, Fassbender inquired about his family, "How's your mom doing?"[8] He also asked about his friends. "Did Travis tell you I talked to him? He seems like a pretty cool kid."[9] Not to be left out, Wiegert got in the mix. "Where does your girlfriend live? . . . Do you talk to her on the Internet or what?"[10]

When things bog down, the topic of the weather is always on standby. "The sky, it looks like it could snow a little bit today," Fassbender said.[11] But Wiegert was more concerned about the freezing rain "that's supposed to come in later. They're sayin' it's supposed to go up to 40-something today."[12] And it helps if the interrogator can actually get the suspect involved in the small talk as well. Wiegert asked, "So, you like snow? . . . Or would you rather have it warm up?"[13] And sometimes it's a good idea to share a personal anecdote to make the interrogator seem more relatable or maybe even human. Wiegert disclosed, "I remember being your age, waitin' for that snow day. That was a, that was a great thing."[14]

And for rapport building, it's also okay to ask questions to which you already know the answer. Wiegert attempted to make a connection by asking, "Do you have to ride the bus to school or, that's, that's how you get to school right?"[15] Throw in a stray comment about a local high school basketball game—"I wonder how bad Menasha got beat"[16]—and the occasional semi-intelligible question about where Dassey has lunch—"You eats lunch at school normally, er?"[17]—and you're off to the races. You have warmed up the suspect and built the appropriate level of rapport. It is now show time. Let the interrogation begin.

Part III
INSIDE THE INTERROGATION ROOM

I I

SCARED STRAIGHT

In season one of AMC's *Better Call Saul*, an ambulance-chasing lawyer named Jimmy wants to represent a man who is about to be charged with embezzlement. So Jimmy meets with the would-be client and his wife, Betsy, to discuss the terms of the potential representation. Betsy, however, was less than impressed; she wanted to retain a different lawyer. So shortly after their disastrous first meeting, Jimmy hatched a scheme to win her over. He recruited two brothers—men even shadier than he was—to stage an accident: one would get hit by Betsy when she was driving her car, and the other would witness it.

When Betsy gets out of the car to see if the man she hit was okay, the brother that was "hit" would continue the scam by faking an injury. The two brothers would then threaten her and extort money from her. This would, of course, send Betsy into full-blown hysteria. But luckily for her, lawyer Jimmy would just so happen to be passing by and would swoop in to save the day. Jimmy would play hardball with the two men (his coconspirators), get them to back down, and impress Betsy with his toughness and legal acumen. And of course, after he gets her out of this fabricated legal problem, she would want to hire him for her husband's *real* legal problem.

The key to the entire scam, of course, is that Jimmy and his coconspirators first have to scare the living daylights out of Betsy, thus creating something from which Jimmy can save her. Spoiler alert: Jimmy's plan was not successful. But unfortunately, this crooked scheme isn't just a worn-out movie trope; it's also a common police interrogation tactic—a tactic Wiegert and Fassbender used to great effect when putting the screws to their sixteen-year-old target.

In interrogation parlance, this tactic is called "maximization." In other words, "the interrogator tries to scare and intimidate the suspect . . . by making false claims about evidence and exaggerating the seriousness of the offense and the magnitude of the charges" that the suspect could be facing.[1] Then, after the suspect is scared straight, the interrogator offers to save the suspect from the fictional problem the interrogator himself created.

Wiegert and Fassbender's maximization ploy—if we want to be generous and connect it to some objective reality—was arguably rooted in Dassey's earlier statement to the two Marinette detectives.[2] As explained in chapter 4, one of the reasons Wiegert and Fassbender eventually targeted Dassey is that some of the things he said to the Marinette detectives "just didn't seem to fit."[3] And it is true that Dassey left the interrogators a bit of an opening in that earlier statement.

For example, fearing that his uncle, Steven Avery, might be wrongfully accused and convicted of yet another crime, Dassey first told the Marinette detectives that he did *not* see Halbach when he got off his school bus on Halloween in 2005. He then admitted to seeing her, but insisted that she got in her truck and drove away from the Avery property as he was walking home.

Arguably, parts of Dassey's statement to the Marinette detectives could have formed the basis for an "obstructing an officer" allegation.[4] While the police are allowed to lie to us citizens with impunity, the reverse is not true and, in fact, can be a crime. But when Wiegert and Fassbender isolated Dassey in their makeshift interrogation room at the high school on February 27, 2006, they began their maximization strategy by "exaggerating the seriousness of the offense" that Dassey could be facing.[5]

Instead of telling Dassey that he could face an "obstructing an officer" charge based on the inconsistencies in his statement to the Marinette detectives, Wiegert and Fassbender told him that he was looking at far more serious charges. Specifically, regarding Halbach's murder and the burning of her corpse, they told Dassey that *he* "could potentially be facing charges for that."[6]

Obviously, nothing Dassey said to the Marinette detectives could possibly have connected him to Halbach's murder, the burning of her corpse, or even the cover-up of those crimes. If Dassey had said anything linking himself to those crimes in any way, the Marinette detectives would have taken him straight to lockup instead of back home after their interrogation in 2005. Nonetheless, Wiegert and Fassbender exaggerated the potential charges. They managed to take the sixteen-year-old's inconsistent statements made to the Marinette detectives—including his statement denying knowledge that was obviously intended to stop the questioning without having to rudely say, "I'm not answering your questions"—and turn those statements into possible murder-related charges.

But how could Wiegert and Fassbender have made such a false allegation against Dassey without any evidence? And how could such a threat even work? After all, there was about as much evidence against Dassey for murder as there was against prosecutor Ken Kratz: in a word, none. Fortunately for Wiegert and Fassbender, they were trained that the maximization tactic involves not only exaggerating the potential criminal charges against a suspect, but also "making false claims about evidence" that supports those charges.[7]

For example, Dassey had told Wiegert and Fassbender that, when he was at Avery's bonfire, he and Avery threw an old car seat into the flames. This was the opening that Fassbender needed. "I gotta believe you did see something in the fire. You wanna know why I believe that? Because Teresa's bones were intermingled in that seat. And the only way her bones were intermingled in that seat is if she was put on that seat" after the seat was placed on the fire.[8]

Obviously, that is not true. First, what does it even mean for something to be "intermingled in [a] seat"? And second, even assuming that "Teresa's bones were intermingled in that seat," they could have become "intermingled" in numerous ways other than Avery and Dassey putting her corpse on top. And even assuming that *Avery* was guilty, the corpse could have been placed on the seat long after Dassey left the bonfire and went home.

But this was just one form of evidence exaggeration deployed by Wiegert and Fassbender, who were, in this regard, able to get away with metaphorical murder. Because Dassey was a child, and they were adult authority figures, they knew Dassey would believe whatever they told him. This allowed them to repeatedly exaggerate the strength of their case without even bothering to make up any details. For example, they repeatedly told Dassey things like "we've got a lot of information," "there's no doubt about it," and "the evidence speaks for itself."[9]

Dassey's interrogators also made statements like this: "We know you saw something," but "you've tried to block it out."[10] This is an especially effective strategy when the suspect is not only a child, but also has "a bad memory."[11] And not only are children and persons with bad memories at greater risk of falsely confessing,[12] but telling such a vulnerable suspect that the evidence proves he saw something (and that he is repressing the memory) is particularly dangerous. "Controlled studies have found that the presentation of manufactured evidence dramatically increases the likelihood that an individual will falsely confess and, at times, even internalize blame for the act."[13]

In short, Wiegert and Fassbender were able to accomplish what the ambulance-chasing lawyer in *Better Call Saul* could not: they successfully scared the living daylights out of their target. They convinced Dassey that he was facing murder-related charges—when, at worst, he was looking at an obstructing charge—and that the evidence against him was strong. The hard work was done. Now all they had to do was to rescue Dassey from the fake problem they had just concocted.

12

PROMISES, PROMISES

If the interrogator has used the "maximization" tactic properly, the suspect will not only be terrified, but will also feel a sense of helplessness. The suspect will believe he is about to be charged with serious crimes and that the government has an airtight case. Neither of these things is true of course—if the police had an airtight case they wouldn't be wasting their time talking to the suspect in the interrogation room—but the suspect believes he is doomed.

At this point, the interrogator puts on a new hat: that of savior. It's time to rescue the suspect from the fake problem the interrogator himself created. It's time to offer a ray of hope, a lifeline, a way out. How? By promising the suspect that cooperating will result in leniency and may even get him out of trouble completely.

But there's one minor roadblock. Strictly speaking, promises are not allowed inside the interrogation room. In order for the prosecutor to later use the confession at trial, the suspect's decision to confess must have been a free and voluntary choice.[1] If, however, the suspect relied on the interrogator's false promises when deciding to confess, those false promises would have made it "impossible for [the suspect] to weigh the pros and cons of confessing."[2] And without being able to weigh the pros and cons, the decision to confess would not have been voluntary. Instead, the confession would be considered involuntary (coerced), and the prosecutor would not be able to use it at trial to convict the suspect-turned-defendant.

Fortunately for the police, however, only *strictly* speaking are promises not allowed. In reality, there are two ways the police are trained to get around this rather soft prohibition. The first way is very similar to the police tactic for getting suspects to waive their Miranda rights. Chapter 9 explained how the police first tell suspects, as required by Miranda, that "anything you say can be used against you." But as soon as they utter those words, they immediately negate the message by repeatedly telling the suspect the exact opposite: that making a statement won't hurt you and, in fact, talking to them will actually help you.

So how does this sleight of hand work in the context of interrogation promises? It's simple. The interrogators first tell the suspect they can't make him any promises, and then they start making promises. For example, before beginning one interrogation, Wiegert told Dassey, "We can't make any promises but we'll stand behind you no matter what you did."[3] Even assuming that the promise to "stand behind you no matter what you did" is somehow not a promise, it wasn't long before Wiegert and Fassbender unleashed a torrent of unequivocal promises powerful enough to induce Dassey to confess.

The second way that interrogators get past the no-promises guideline is to rely on this Wisconsin Court of Appeals doublespeak: "An officer telling a defendant that his cooperation would be to his benefit is not coercive conduct, at least so long as leniency is not promised."[4] This makes no sense, of course, as the only "benefit" a suspect could possibly be thinking about while sitting in an interrogation room and being accused of a crime is "leniency." Nonetheless, this nonsensical distinction provides interrogators with a way to legally make false promises to induce the suspect to confess. And Wiegert and Fassbender took full advantage of this rule when extracting a confession from their target.

Dassey's interrogators started things off by reinforcing that sense of helplessness. They made clear that Dassey was in deep water and they were the only ones who could help him. As we saw in the earlier Miranda-related chapters, they told Dassey that "people back at the sheriff's department" and "district attorney's office" wanted to file charges against him for Halbach's murder, but they—Wiegert and Fassbender—were holding them at bay.[5] Fassbender was as clear as he was untruthful: "Mark and I are both going well, ah, he's a kid, he had nothing to do with this."[6] They also made Dassey believe that his own family members had turned against him.

> Steve doesn't care about you right now, he cares about himself. Unfortunately that's all Steven cares about. He left you to hang out to dry. . . . You're the only one that we talked to between the other brothers, Blain, Bobby, Bryan, that is inconsistent with what they said.[7]

And now Dassey was primed for their promises. Wiegert and Fassbender wanted to show Dassey what they could do for him. "We wanna go back and tell people that, you know . . . Brendan was honest, he's not like Steve, he's honest, he's a good guy."[8] So they repeatedly used an analogy to hammer away at their point. "Mark and I both can go back to the district attorney and say, ah, Dassey came forward and finally told us. . . . We'll *go to bat for ya*, but you have to be honest with us."[9] More specifically, "honesty" is whatever pleases the interrogators: "I'm your friend right now, *but I . . . gotta believe in you and if I don't believe in you* I can't go to bat for you."[10]

Fearing that Dassey might not grasp the baseball metaphor, Wiegert and Fassbender used a variation on a biblical theme that Dassey would be able to take literally, but the trial judge and appellate court could later dismiss as mere figure of speech rather than a promise. They told him, "Honesty is the only thing *that will set you free*."[11] Not only was this a promise, but, as Dassey's post-conviction lawyers pointed out, it was a false one.

> Plainly, the officers overcame Brendan's reluctance only by assuring him that everything would be all right as long as he confessed. But in reality, the opposite was true: because no witness or physical evidence linked Brendan to Halbach's rape or murder, Brendan was safe from legal jeopardy *unless* he confessed.[12]

And just in case both the baseball analogy and the biblical reference were lost on the learning-disabled child, the interrogators got very specific with their promises of leniency—the exact thing that the law, in theory, prohibits. As Dassey's post-conviction counsel argued:

> It is unreasonable to assert . . . that Brendan's interrogators made no false promises of leniency. . . . The videotape reflects many such promises, including that even if Brendan made "statements against your own interest," then "from what I'm seeing I'm thinkin' you're all right. OK, you don't have to worry about things"; "honesty here is the thing that's gonna help you"; "by you talking with us, it's, it's helping you"; "no matter what you did, we can work through that"; "the honest person is the one who's gonna get a better deal out of everything"; and "if, in fact, you did some things, which we believe it's OK. As long as you [can] be

honest with us, it's OK. If you lie about it that's gonna be problems."
. . . "Let's get it all out today and this will be all over with."[13]

In short, "It is fictional to believe that such message[s] of leniency did not affect Brendan's decision to talk" rather than to remain silent.[14] Worse yet, the above messages are only a few handpicked examples from the multiple hours of interrogations. Readers may have even noticed that the above passage—and a few other passages in this book so far—are unavoidably repetitive. And this gives some insight into how Dassey must have felt, as promises of leniency were "repeated *twenty* times on February 27" and "similar promises of leniency were made *twenty-one* times" during the March 1 interrogation.[15]

Wiegert and Fassbender's message to Dassey was coming through forcefully and frequently: he would receive leniency, and even escape punishment entirely, if he just confessed. So Dassey took their deal. And there was no doubt that he did so in order to receive the leniency he was promised—including that if he got "it all out today" then "this will be all over with." After Dassey gave his interrogators what they had asked for, he expected them to make good on their end of the bargain and take him back to school. He asked Wiegert, "Do you think I can get there before one twenty-nine? . . . I have a project due in sixth hour."[16]

Oops, Brendan. Brendan wasn't going anywhere—or at least not back to school. As explained in chapter 1, he had just confessed to murder, along with rape and corpse mutilation for good measure.

But wait! You may be thinking that the interrogators didn't make promises to get Dassey to confess; rather, they technically made promises to get the truth, regardless of what the truth was. And if the truth was that Dassey didn't know or do anything, then he should have said that.

Actually, Dassey did say that. But Wiegert and Fassbender weren't going to let his claims of innocence get in the way of a confession. Besides, what is truth, anyway? As the next chapter explains, it's whatever Wiegert and Fassbender say it is.

13

WORDPLAY

What does the word "truth" mean? What does any word mean, really? In police- and prosecutor-speak, the definitions of words are not fixed; rather, they are flexible. This way, words can take on whatever meaning best suits the government at any given point in time.

My favorite example of this wordplay comes from the case *State v. Locke*,[1] where a Wisconsin prosecutor cut a plea deal with a defendant. The defendant agreed to plead guilty to two crimes, and the prosecutor agreed to refrain from making a specific recommendation as to the length of the sentence the court should impose. The prosecutor would still be allowed to say all the bad things he wanted about the defendant at the sentencing hearing. The prosecutor was merely obligated not to recommend a specific number of years in prison.

So what did the prosecutor do? After getting the defendant to plead guilty, he violated his end of the bargain by specifically recommending the maximum sentence of fifty years. According to the prosecutor, however, this wasn't a specific recommendation. Actually, the prosecutor argued, it wasn't a recommendation at all.

We all know what the word "recommendation" means, but the prosecutor simply changed its meaning to suit the government's needs. When he told the judge he should dole out a fifty-year sentence, that was not a recommendation; it was a non-recommendation. More specifically, the prosecutor had the gall to say in open court, "So the recommendation here is a *non-recommendation* as far as what I can say to lock Mr. Locke—lock Mr. Locke—up for fifty years, with thirty years of initial confinement and fifty [*sic*] years of extended supervision."[2]

To begin, the prosecutor was so excited by his play on words— "lock" and "Locke"—that he lost the ability to perform basic arithmetic. The appellate court observed that, to arrive at a fifty-year sentence that includes thirty years of initial confinement, "[t]he most reasonable inter-pretation of the prosecutor's statement is that it was a recommendation for only a twenty-year term of extended supervision."[3] But second, and more important, the prosecutor reneged on his agreement not to make a spe-cific sentencing recommendation, and then tried to hoodwink the court by changing the meaning of the word "recommendation." And, to give the prosecutor full credit for his creativity, he also coined some new legal terminology in the process: "the *non*-recommendation recommendation."[4]

But this kind of wordplay is not unique to prosecutors; it's a favorite ploy of the police, too. In fact, Wiegert and Fassbender used this tactic to great effect when, during their multiple interrogations of Dassey, they redefined the words "truth" and "honesty." Dr. Lawrence T. White, the false confession expert featured in *Making a Murderer*, put it this way:

> The two detectives develop this theme of honesty, and they repeat-edly, dozens of times in that [March 1, 2006 interrogation], they say to Brendan, "Now be honest. You know how important it is to be honest." But when you watch the videotapes, it's clear . . . that when they say to Brendan "be honest," what they sort of mean is "don't tell us *that*, tell us something else"—something that fits their theory of the crime.[5]

But given that most people, including Dassey, know what the words truth and honesty mean, it takes a lot of work for Wiegert and Fassbender to change the meaning of those words in Dassey's mind. To begin, they use the words in a general sense, getting Dassey's buy-in that truth and honesty are good things. For example, at one point they tell Dassey, "We'll go to bat for ya, but you have to be honest with us. . . . I promise I will not let you hang out there, but we've gotta have the truth."[6] As another example, they warn him, "As long as you can, as long as you be honest with us, it's OK. If you lie about it that's gonna be problems. OK. Does that sound fair?"[7]

Next, it's time to change the meanings of the two words. Whenever Dassey gives an answer the interrogators don't like, they simply let him know that he is not being honest and that his answer is not the truth. After Dassey has been held captive for many hours over two days, and hears their rebukes dozens of times, the words eventually lose their real meaning and instead become synonymous with whatever makes his interrogators happy.

For example, when Wiegert and Fassbender asked Dassey what he saw in Avery's bonfire on the night of Halbach's disappearance, he said, "Some black—some garbage bag on there."[8] Obviously, because the interrogators wanted Dassey to have seen Halbach's remains, they rejected the answer: "you have to tell the truth."[9] Eventually, after a lengthy prodding to be honest, Dassey came around to his interrogators' version of the truth, now claming to have seen Halbach's clothing, and even her remains, in the fire.

As another example, when the interrogators were working on their timeline, they asked Dassey if the fire was already started when he got to Avery's home on Halloween. He replied, "No it wasn't."[10] This, however, did not fit the version of events the interrogators had constructed. Fassbender stated, "We're not gonna go any further in this cuz we need to get the truth out now. We know the fire was going. . . . Let's talk it through honestly now."[11] Wiegert added, "Come on Brendan. Be honest. I told you before that's the only thing that's gonna help ya here. We already know what happened."[12]

Wiegert and Fassbender also wanted to rope Dassey into Halbach's actual murder, rather than just the burning of her corpse. So they needed to place Dassey inside Avery's trailer. Fassbender urged, "OK, let's, to this point now, I think we're *pretty close to the truth*."[13] But when Dassey said he didn't go inside the trailer, Wiegert responded, "Come on now. . . . Be honest. You went inside, didn't you?"[14]

This was a recurring theme throughout all of Dassey's interrogations. As far back as November 6, 2005, when the two Marinette detectives got Dassey in the back of their squad car, government agents had been putting up the same, tired façade: they were there to help Dassey, and they only wanted the truth—unless, of course, the truth didn't match their version of events.

For example, when Dassey told the Marinette detectives that he got off the school bus and saw Halbach leaving Avery's property in her vehicle, the detectives rejected that account because it didn't fit with their theory that Avery had her (or her corpse) somewhere on his property. Their exchange with Dassey then went as follows:

Det. Baldwin: Brendan, I know you're scared, okay. I understand that, all right. I want to try to help you, okay.

Dassey: Yeah, what, take Steven away from me?

Det. Baldwin: No.

Dassey: Like 18 years again?

Det. Baldwin: Bottom line is, we don't want that to happen. . . . And nobody's sayin' that Steven did this, okay, nobody's sayin' that. But to get beyond Steven, we have to know *the truth* okay. So why don't you tell me what happened to her? . . . I know you're still not tellin' me *the truth* cuz I know your, you look all choked up to me . . . You look like you want to tell me somethin' else. Like *the truth*.[15]

Ironically, all of Dassey's interrogators—O'Neill, Baldwin, Wiegert, and Fassbender—repeatedly claimed to want honesty and truth, yet many of their own claims were flat-out lies. They repeatedly lied about their motives, what they knew, what other people had said, whom they were targeting, and whom they were trying to help. And the unsettling part is that they all seemed to lie so effortlessly. The audio and video revealed no apparent inner struggle in a moral sense, and certainly no practical difficulty when formulating their falsehoods.

For example, when the scared sixteen-year-old tells Baldwin that he's worried about his uncle being taken away from him, Baldwin is cool as November in Wisconsin when he assures the child that no one is targeting his uncle as the perpetrator. Similarly, as Wiegert and Fassbender are leading the boy down the path toward life imprisonment, they clearly tell him that they are on his side and are even protecting him from other government agents.

Given this, it is not unreasonable to wonder whether these detectives can really switch back-and-forth from lie-telling mode to truth-telling mode, or whether the truth has become blurred for them. In other words, they seem to lie to Dassey so easily and so often that perhaps they actually believe what they are selling him. If that is the case, then "the truth" really is whatever the interrogators want it to be.

14

IT'S BETTER TO GIVE THAN TO RECEIVE

Wiegert and Fassbender had convinced themselves that they knew exactly what happened on Halloween in 2005. Their next step was to convince Dassey. If Dassey wasn't convinced, he might not be willing to agree with the version of events they were foisting upon him.

Selling a suspect on an interrogator's special ability to divine the truth isn't always an easy task. One of my former clients, when confronted by an interrogator who claimed to already know what happened, logically responded: "Great, if you already know, then you don't need to question me." Much to the detective's chagrin, that particular interrogation ended before it could even get off the ground.

But fortunately for Wiegert and Fassbender, they were dealing with a much easier target: a learning-disabled child who had no experience with the police and had no idea that lying is a detective's stock in trade. So nearly every time they prodded Dassey for "the truth" or to "be honest," they also told him that they "already knew" the answer they wanted. For example, in the interrogation at the Manitowoc Sheriff's Department,

> the interrogators rejected Brendan's attempts to deny involvement and told him *twenty-four times* that they *already knew* what he had done. The message was unmistakable, especially for a mentally limited sixteen-year-old: Brendan was clearly led to believe that he would not be punished for telling them the incriminating details they professed to *already know*.[1]

From a logistical standpoint, however, there was a sticking point: Dassey didn't have access to the facts that his interrogators "professed to already know." Therefore, Wiegert and Fassbender had to provide the details that would eventually make up the confession. They would have preferred it if Dassey could come up with the details himself, so they often gave him the opportunity to first guess what they wanted to hear. Eventually, though, they had to fill in the blanks for him, and then get his agreement to the facts they had just fed him.

In a now-famous example of this tactic, Wiegert and Fassbender believed that Halbach had been shot in the head. It was therefore important that Dassey admit either to shooting her or seeing Avery shoot her. This way, his confession would be consistent with the state's theory—and, in this particular instance, with the evidence—thus increasing the odds of a guilty verdict at trial. Their exchange went as follows:

Wiegert: What else did he do to her? We know something else was done. Tell us, and what else did you do? Come on. *Something with the head*. Brendan? . . .

Fassbender: We have the evidence Brendan, we just need you ta, ta be honest with us.

Brendan: That he cut off her hair. . . .

Fassbender: *What else was done to her head?*

Brendan: That he punched her.

Wiegert: What else? What else? . . .

Brendan: Cut her. . . . On her throat. . . .

Fassbender: It's extremely, extremely important you tell us this, for us to believe you.

Wiegert: Come on Brendan, what else?

Fassbender: We know, we just need you to tell us.

Brendan: That's all I can remember.

Wiegert: All right, I'm just gonna come out and ask you. *Who shot her in the head?*

Brendan: He did.

Fassbender: Then why didn't you tell us that?

Brendan: Cuz I couldn't think of it.[2]

Although Dassey adopted the interrogators' facts, this type of exchange isn't the best material for the prosecutor to work with at trial.

The risk, from the state's perspective, is that the defense lawyer will argue that Dassey never really said that Halbach was shot in the head. Rather, he was given multiple guesses and couldn't come up with the answer, which obviously means that he wasn't there when Halbach was killed. Then, the defense lawyer might argue, it was the interrogators who fed Dassey the answer they wanted—that Halbach was shot in the head—and Dassey, once again, simply agreed with them.

The interrogators knew this was a risk, so they tried to at least make it look like they weren't giving Dassey the answers they wanted to hear. This required a little game of "we're not telling you what to say, but . . . ." For example, after much shaping and molding of the story, Wiegert and Fassbender got Dassey to say that, when he got off the school bus on Halloween of 2005, he saw Avery and Halbach outside on Avery's porch, and he saw Halbach's car parked outside as well.

This was certainly better for the state than Dassey's original statement that he saw Halbach driving away from the alleged scene of her murder. However, it still didn't fit the interrogators' timeline. They believed that, by the time Dassey got off his school bus, Halbach was already inside, not outside, of Avery's trailer. And they also believed her car was already inside, not outside, of Avery's garage. These were critical points, so they told Dassey what they wanted, but without telling him what they wanted. Fassbender was all but winking at Dassey when he delivered this monologue:

> Mark and I are havin' a problem with that. . . . I'm not, *I'm not sayin'*
> *that I'm gonna put words in your mouth*, so I'm havin' a problem with
> that. You know, Blain not seeing [Halbach and her car] and stuff like
> that. . . . Is there somethin' you need to tell us about that? When you
> got home what did you see before you went into your house? . . . [T]he
> time periods aren't adding up. . . . Um, and, and I know, *I guarantee ya*
> *Teresa's not standing on that porch when you come home from school.* . . . Ya,
> *I have a problem with the car sittin' out front yet at this time.* . . . Somethin'
> is not adding up here and you need to tell us the truth. . . . *I can't tell you*
> *these things.* I *can* tell ya we don't believe you . . .[3]

Brendan gets the message loud and clear about what Fassbender is (not) telling him to say. Fassbender has just "guaranteed" that Halbach and her jeep were not outside when Dassey arrived home. So Dassey changes his story as requested.

Brendan: I got off the bus. I walked down the road and when I got to that thing . . . I could see her jeep *in the garage* just sittin' there and I *didn't* see Steven and her on the, the porch.

Wiegert: You, you did or you didn't?

Brendan: I didn't.

Fassbender: Did not, OK.[4]

Fassbender essentially, if not literally, said this: Brendan, I can't tell you to say they were inside the trailer. But I *can* call you a liar for saying they were outside the trailer. Similarly—are you still with me Brendan?—I can't tell you to say that the car was inside the garage. But I *can* call you a liar for saying that it was parked outside the garage. Now, tell us the truth.

Of course, Brendan gives them exactly what they are demanding. And just like that, Avery and Halbach went from being outside to being inside the trailer, and Halbach's car went from being outside to being inside the garage. Now the facts are starting to fit the state's theory of the case—"the truth."

This fact feeding was par for the course. All of Dassey's interrogations consisted of the detectives giving, rather than receiving, information. For example, Wiegert needed Dassey to say that Avery had taken the license plates off Halbach's vehicle. Dassey didn't see this, of course, so Wiegert simply told him.

Wiegert: OK. After he put the car there, what do you do next?

Brendan: We walk out.

Wiegert: With, how's, the license plates were taken off the car, who did that?

Brendan: I don't know.

Wiegert: Did you do that?

Brendan: No.

Wiegert: Did Steve do that?

Brendan: Yeah.

Wiegert: Well then why'd you say you don't know? Did Steve take the license plates off the car?

Brendan: Yeah.[5]

Similarly, Fassbender believed that Avery had gone under the hood of Halbach's vehicle—an important fact for the state. It was easy to get Dassey to agree.

> Fassbender: OK, what else did he do, he did somethin' else, you need to tell us what he did, after that car is parked there. It's extremely important. Before you guys leave that car.
>
> Brendan: He left the gun in the car.
>
> Fassbender: That's not what I'm thinkin' about. He did something to that car. He took the plates and he, I believe he did something else in that car.
>
> Brendan: I don't know.
>
> Fassbender: OK. Did he, did he, did he go and look at the engine, did he raise the hood at all or anything like that? To do something to that car?
>
> Brendan: Yeah.[6]

And the interrogators were using this tactic from the get-go. Traveling back in time to the Mishicot High School interrogation, did Dassey really say that he saw body parts in the fire? Sort of, but only after repeatedly denying it, and then being fed the following details by Fassbender:

> Tell us what you saw. You saw some body parts. You're shaking your head. Tell us what you saw. . . . You all right? You all right? What other parts did you see? . . . Did you see part of the *arm*, the *legs*? I know. It's alright. Did you see part of her *head*? *Skull*?[7]

And this portion of the interrogation actually demonstrates a larger point. It's obvious from Fassbender's comments—"You all right? You all right?"—that Dassey was getting overwhelmed by this gruesome line of questioning. For this and other reasons, interrogators shouldn't go too far too fast with a suspect. As the next chapter explains, instead of trying to go from zero to full confession in five seconds flat, the better interrogation tactic is to move slowly, but steadily, toward the confession—one baby step at a time.

15

BABY STEPS

A good interrogator doesn't come barreling out of the gates by asking the suspect, "Did you do the crime?" That's too much, too soon. One of the dangers of such a direct approach is that the suspect could get scared—sooner than the interrogator wants him to—and might refuse to cooperate. But when O'Neill, Baldwin, Wiegert, and Fassbender made the mistake of being too aggressive too soon with Dassey, they got bailed out. Because they were working in pairs against an overmatched child who never mustered the courage to tell them to pound sand, the interrogators' sloppiness didn't hurt them.

However, it is also true that when Dassey's interrogators asked too much too soon, they didn't get anywhere. Instead, their success came when they took baby steps—slowly and gradually, but steadily, leading Dassey to prison. To stick with the baseball theme that Wiegert and Fassbender loved to use—they had repeatedly promised to "go to bat" for Dassey—the interrogators enjoyed much more success when they went for singles and the occasional extra-base hit instead of swinging for the fences. Wiegert was partially correct when he testified at trial:

> Well, obviously, when you keep learning little bits and pieces, Brendan keeps telling us *a little more here, a little more there*, we realized it could probably be either [he] saw more, knew more, something. We need to make arrangements to go back and talk to him again. That was obvious.[1]

Wiegert was accurate to say that the story was developed a little bit at time. However, it wasn't Brendan who was giving the information to his interrogators. Rather, as the previous chapter demonstrated, it was the interrogators who were giving the information—"a little more here, a little more there"—to Brendan.

As Dassey's lawyers argued, his statements were "the result of . . . repeated leading and suggestive questioning"[2]—the type of questioning that causes children, and even many adults, to falsely confess. Further, Dassey's lawyers argued, the state "is flagrantly wrong to characterize the interrogation as a litany of open-ended questions[.]"[3] Rather, the interrogation consisted of "[d]ozens of leading questions . . . *each advancing the story another step*."[4]

It was this incremental approach of leading Dassey down the primrose path—combined with the interrogators' scare tactics, reassuring promises, and wordplay with "truth" and "honesty"—that eventually formed Dassey's confession. And it all started with baby step number one. The interrogators first had to get Dassey to admit something small: that he saw a body in the flames. And even this much took baby steps.

> Fassbender: Brendan, we know that, that Halloween and stuff you were with him and, and helped him tend to a fire . . . anything that you saw that night that's been bothering ya? . . . What did you see in the fire?
>
> Brendan: Some branches, a cabinet, and some tires. . . .
>
> Fassbender: You know if you think you saw something in the fire . . . I gotta believe you did see something in the fire. . . . Truthfully, I don't believe Steven intended to kill her. . . . What did you see in that fire?
>
> Brendan: Some black—some garbage bag on there. . . .[5]

Now it was time to move Dassey forward a step or two, which resulted in him seeing some clothing.

> Fassbender: I don't think Steven intended to do it, but it happened. . . . I'm afraid you saw something . . . and that's what we need to know. We get that off your chest and we can move forward. . . .[6]
>
> Wiegert: I find it quite difficult to believe that if there was a body in that, Brendan, that you wouldn't have seen something. . . . We know you saw something. And maybe you've tried to block it out . . .
>
> Fassbender: It's OK, it's a big step, a step toward feeling better about yourself . . . what you saw.
>
> Brendan: Some clothes like a blue shirt, some pants.[7]

Once Dassey said he saw clothing, it was a small step to get him to say there was blood on that clothing.

Wiegert: Was there blood on those clothes? Be honest Brendan. We know. We already know you know. Help us out. . . . Was there blood on those clothes?

Brendan: A little bit. . . .[8]

And once there is blood, there must be body parts, right? It should be easy to take that step, provided Dassey is reassured that he's not to blame.

Fassbender: Yeah, it's not your fault. . . . You know we found some flesh in that fire too. We know you saw some flesh. . . . Tell us. You saw some body parts. You're shaking your head. Tell us what you saw.

Brendan: Toes . . . forehead . . . a little flesh.[9]

Now the body parts just need to be connected, which will create the entire body. The hip bone is connected to the leg bone, which is connected to the foot bone, and so on.

Wiegert: Were all the body parts connected yet? Yes? Did you say yes or no? I'm not sure.

Brendan: Yeah.

Fassbender: So all the body parts were pretty much connected then when you saw the toes, which means they were probably connected to the feet yet, correct? Which means the feet, foot is connected to both legs, so I'm just going to ask this question . . . You're pretty much, you're seeing a body? Is that accurate? You saw her body in there?

Wiegert: Would you say yes or no for me Brendan?

Brendan: Yes.[10]

And just like that, Wiegert and Fassbender got Dassey strolling down the path to a full confession. But while seeing a body in the fire is a good start, it is not evidence of murder or even rape. Yet, it was too big of a leap to jump from Dassey merely seeing the body to actually committing the crimes. Therefore, the next baby step was to get Dassey to admit that he helped Avery put the body in the fire.

Wiegert: Brendan, I'm going to ask you a difficult question, OK? Did you help him put that body in the fire? If you did it's OK.

Brendan: [Denies the allegation.][11]

Fassbender: We pretty much know everything, that's why we're talking to you again today. . . . If in fact you did some things, which we believe, some things may have happened that you didn't wanna tell us about. . . .[12]

Wiegert: Let's be honest here Brendan. If you helped him, it's OK, because he was telling you to do it. You didn't do it on your own.

Brendan: I didn't, I didn't touch her. . . .

Wiegert: Why did he, why did he have you come over there? Did he need help with something? Remember, we already know, but we need to hear it from you. Why did he have you come over there? He needed help, didn't he? What did he need help with? Go ahead and tell us.

Brendan: Probably to get rid of the body.

Wiegert: Yeah.[13]

After laboriously feeding and then extracting the details of how the body was disposed of, Wiegert and Fassbender continued to work backward in time. Dassey had admitted to seeing the body in the fire, and then to helping Avery put it there, so the next step was to talk about how Halbach was killed. In theory, this was a relatively easy baby step to take; it only required Dassey to admit that Avery *told* him things, and not that Dassey did anything. But the interrogators believed there was a rape involved too, thus making the extraction a bit more difficult.

Fassbender: Did he try to have sex with her, or anything, and she said no?

Wiegert: Did he ever tell you that? It's very important, OK, cuz we had heard that he might have told you that. No? Yes or no?

Brendan: No. . . .[14]

Wiegert: Did he say anything about sexual assault with, with her, or having sex with her?

Brendan: No.

Wiegert: Did he say anything about wanting to?

Brendan: No. . . .[15]

Wiegert: What else did he do ta her? We already know, be honest. . . . What else did he do ta her?

Brendan: Raped her.

Wiegert: Did he tell you that?

Fassbender: Tell us about that. And where he did it. . . .

Wiegert: What did he say he did, in his words? What did he tell you? You can swear, you can use any of his language you want. Tell us exactly what he told you he did to her. . . .

Brendan: Raped her.

Fassbender: What did he say? Did he use those words?

Wiegert: Are you sure cuz it's not usually the words he uses. Are, are, if you're sure, that's OK.

Brendan: Yeah.[16]

The next baby step is to put Dassey at the scene of the rape and murder, as a witness. If he agrees to being present *for* the crimes, then he's only one step away from admitting his direct involvement *in* the crimes.

Wiegert: Brendan, were you there when this [rape and murder] happened?

Brendan: No.[17]

Fassbender: OK, let's, to this point now, I think we're pretty close to the truth. . . . OK, then give us the little parts that we don't have yet up ta that point. . . . I think you went over to his house and then he asked [you] to get his mail, somethin' in here is missing.

Brendan: Well, when I got the mail there was like a envelope in there with his name on it. . . . I knocked on the door and he answered it. . . . I gave it to him and I left.

Wiegert: Come on now. You just heard screaming over there.

Fassbender: You're making this hard on us and yourself.

Wiegert: Be honest. *You went inside, didn't you?*

Fassbender: Yeah.

Wiegert: You went in the trailer?

Brendan: Mm huh.

Fassbender: You're noddin'.

Wiegert: OK, did you go back there [into Avery's bedroom] and look? . . . Could you see her?

Brendan: Yeah.[18]

From here, he was just a baby step or two away from the full-blown confession. They next got Dassey to say that Avery asked him to join in the sexual assault. Wiegert began, "What happens next? Remember, we already know, but we need to hear it from you, it's OK."[19] Fassbender then jumps in the mix, "Does he ask you?"[20] Then Wiegert says, "He does, doesn't he?"[21] Fassbender reminds Dassey, "We know."[22] Wiegert continues the badgering, "He asks you doesn't he? . . . Come on, be honest, you went back in that room. . . . We know you were back there. Let's get it all out today and this will be all over with."[23]

After getting Dassey to admit to participating in the sexual assault, the interrogators then got him to admit to participating in the actual murder. Wiegert prodded, "You helped to tie her up though, didn't you? Brendan, cuz he couldn't tie her up alone, there's no way. Did you help him tie her up? . . . Go ahead, Bud."[24] They then went on to extract details about how she was tied up, choked, and stabbed—although the details never remained the same from one sentence to the next.

The finishing touch, of course, is to get Dassey to admit that they *shot* Halbach. If Wiegert and Fassbender could accomplish this, it might turn a nonsensical story into a believable confession. At this point—the fourth interrogation in less than forty-eight hours—Dassey would likely have admitted to helping Avery with the Kennedy assassination, if that's what the interrogators wanted. So to make it appear as though the information was coming *from* Dassey, rather than being fed *to* Dassey, they asked him an open-ended question. As discussed in chapter 14, they asked, "What was done to her head?" However, after Dassey's three incorrect guesses, Wiegert's frustration produced the most famous question of the interrogation. "All right, I'm just gonna come out and ask you. Who shot her in the head?"[25]

At this point, Mark, does it really matter?

16

"IT'S NOT YOUR FAULT"

The previous chapters illustrated many of the techniques that Wiegert and Fassbender employed to produce Dassey's confession. But even the government's interrogation machinery, as powerful as it is, can bog down once in a while. Therefore, the interrogators had to apply an occasional dollop of grease to keep it running smoothly. And one of those forms of grease is a tactic called "minimization."

Minimization "is a 'soft sell' technique in which the detective tries to lull the suspect into a false sense of security by offering sympathy, tolerance, face-saving excuses, and moral justification; by blaming the . . . accomplice; and by underplaying the seriousness or magnitude of the charges."[1] And this tactic is highly effective.

> Controlled studies have demonstrated that minimization techniques are effective in persuading guilty suspects to confess. Unfortunately, they also induce some innocent suspects to confess falsely. Indeed, in one realistic simulation, an investigator induced 43 percent of *innocent* suspects to provide a false confession by . . . minimizing the seriousness of the offense by offering sympathy and a face-saving excuse.[2]

So whenever the interrogation would hit a sticking point—a point where Dassey might have been thinking that perhaps talking to his interrogators wasn't such a good idea—Wiegert and Fassbender shifted into minimization mode. From Dassey's perspective, this was a welcomed change and provided temporary relief from the interrogators' equally effective maximization tactics.

The minimization strategy was evident early in the process. As Dassey told the Marinette detectives on November 6, 2005, he was concerned that the police were going to take his Uncle Steven away from him and wrongly imprison him a second time. And Wiegert and Fassbender knew this; as chapter 4 explained, Wiegert testified that he reviewed Dassey's statement to the Marinette detectives before he and Fassbender put the screws to the child on February 27, 2006, at Mishicot High School.

Given this, they began their interrogation of Dassey by minimizing what Avery had done. They offered tolerance and a face-saving excuse for his behavior. "Whether it was an accident that Steven did it . . . truthfully, I don't believe Steven intended to kill her."[3] Then, to get Dassey talking about having seen body parts in the fire, they minimized Dassey's role and shifted the blame toward Avery's conduct, rather than anything Dassey might have done.

> Mark and I are both going well, ah, he's a kid, he had nothing to do with this. And whether Steve got him out there to help build a fire and he inadvertently saw some things, that's what it would be. It wouldn't be that Brendan act-actually helped him dispose of this body.[4]

These minimization tactics were occasionally applied throughout the many interrogations; this form of grease ensured that the false-confession machinery continued to operate and Dassey continued to talk. For example, after he agreed with the interrogators that he had seen clothing, then blood, then body parts, and then the entire body in the fire, Fassbender got a little too confrontational. "And you never said anything to him. Have you told this to anyone?"[5] Realizing he may have gotten too aggressive, he quickly went back to minimization mode. "And is that what's been bothering you a lot? And, and I understand that, that's normal because you've done nothing wrong."[6]

When the interrogators got to each new stage of their questioning, they would use more minimization tactics to keep things rolling. For example, in order to get Dassey to admit that, rather than merely seeing the body in the fire, he actually helped Avery put it there, the interrogators offered Dassey an out by once again minimizing his conduct: "he was telling you to do it."[7] Dassey still denied having assisted Avery, so Fassbender offered a more specific, face-saving excuse. "He used you for this. . . . He threatened you. Tell us that."[8]

Similarly, when the interrogators wanted to move from getting Dassey to say that he helped dispose of the body to saying that he raped Halbach, Avery was once again the bad guy. Wiegert began, "He brings you back there and he shows you her and what do you do? . . . It's not your fault, he makes you do it."[9] Dassey won't yet admit to the rape, so Fassbender joins in, making Avery, rather than Dassey, the focus. "What does Steven make you do?"[10]

Likewise, when it comes time for the interrogators to nudge Dassey from the rape to the murder, it is Avery, not Dassey, who is to blame. Wiegert began, "We know something else was done. Tell us, and what else did you do? Come on."[11] To induce a response, Fassbender offered the now-familiar moral bailout. "What he made you do Brendan, we know he made you do somethin' else."[12] Fassbender continued, stressing that the devil, so to speak, made Dassey do it. "He made you do some-thin' to her, didn't he? So he-he would feel better about not bein' the only person, right? Yeah. . . . What did he make you do to her?"[13] Wiegert hammered home the message. "What did he make you do Brendan? It's OK, what did he make you do?"[14]

When viewed in isolation, some of these minimization tactics look incredibly absurd. Going back to the very first tactic where the interroga-tors minimized Avery's alleged murder as an "accident," some suspects might have thought or even said, "Really, Mark and Tom? You think that if Avery murdered that woman and burned her corpse it was just 'an accident'? And you 'truthfully' believe that Avery did not intend to do those things? If that is your idea of 'truth,' then there's no point in talking to you and I am ending this interrogation right now."

In fact, when Wiegert and Fassbender tried this accident-themed interrogation on Steven Avery, it failed miserably. Stepping away, momentarily, from Dassey's case, consider Avery's stationhouse inter-rogation right before his formal arrest. Avery knew that the face-saving "accident" excuse Wiegert and Fassbender were selling him was absurd. They began by asking him, "How long were you put away for, did ya say?" referring to his wrongful conviction and eighteen-year imprisonment in the Penny Beerntsen rape case.[15] "Was that rough on ya? . . . I understand that. . . . That kinda screws a guy up a little bit."[16] Then, with regard to the Halbach murder and corpse burning, they offered Avery a way out. "Hey, if this was an accident, I don't think you meant for this to happen. . . . It was probably a mistake. It was most likely a mistake."[17]

They then confronted Avery with fabricated evidence and other bald-faced lies, telling him that Halbach's blood and DNA were found inside his trailer (none was), that they had obtained his bloody palm print (they hadn't), that a bloodhound had retraced his precise movements during the crime (it hadn't), and that the Manitowoc County Sheriff's Department—which was potentially on the hook in Avery's civil lawsuit—had nothing whatsoever to do with finding Halbach's car key in his bedroom (it had). This overwhelming "evidence," they insisted, left Avery with only two choices: "It's just a matter of did you do this intentionally or was it an accident?"[18]

They tried to persuade Avery that, if he admitted to accidentally killing Halbach and burning her corpse, that would be okay. However, "If it's not a mistake, that makes you a cold-blooded killer. If it's a mistake, then I understand it. The judge understands. The jury understands. . . . But if it's not a mistake, that means it's intentional and you're a cold-blooded killer."[19]

Avery refused to buy either one of the choices his interrogators were selling. And regardless of one's opinion of his actual guilt or innocence, this much is undeniable: Avery offered Wiegert and Fassbender a far more plausible explanation than the "accidental" murder theory they were pushing. Avery said, "I didn't do it. Someone's doin' a good job on me."[20]

POSITIVE FEEDBACK

Positive feedback is a powerful tool. Consider its use in the context of eyewitness identifications. Most jurors associate an eyewitness's confidence level with the accuracy of his identification. That is, the more confident the witness was when he picked the defendant out of a lineup, the more likely the jury is to find the defendant guilty. However,

> confidence can be increased artificially. For example, positive feedback from an officer after the identification procedure will reaffirm the witness's choice, thereby increasing confidence. This type of feedback from police . . . not only inflates the eyewitness's confidence level, but studies have shown that it also "leads them to report that they had a better view of the culprit, that they could make out details of the face . . . that their memorial image of the [person was] particularly clear, and that they are adept at recognizing faces of strangers."[1]

Staying with this example of eyewitness identification for a moment, recall the three identification procedures that the Manitowoc County Sheriff's Department administered for Penny Beerntsen, the victim in Avery's first conviction in the mid-1980s. The deputies had her identify Avery as the perpetrator three times: first in a single sketch show-up procedure, then in a photo-array procedure, and then in a line-up procedure. Given how badly the deputies wanted Avery to be guilty of that crime, it would not be surprising if they had praised Beerntsen and unleashed the confetti after each of her three positive identifications. Such positive feedback would certainly account for her high confidence level when she falsely identified Avery in court.

If positive feedback from the police can have such a dramatic effect on adults in the context of an eyewitness identification procedure—a situation where the feedback can literally alter the witness's memory of the event—imagine the impact that positive feedback would have on a scared, isolated, highly suggestible, learning-disabled child with a bad memory.

Just as Wiegert and Fassbender used "minimization" as a form of grease to keep the interrogation machinery running smoothly, so too did they use positive feedback for that same purpose. They would praise Dassey every time he said something, or even headed in a general direction, of which they approved. For example, after the Mishicot High School interrogation, they knew they would want more statements—four more, as it turned out, with the fifth statement coming after the state filed its criminal complaint and Dassey was represented by Len Kachinsky. So Fassbender doled out some positive feedback for the child's performance up to that point.

> I want to say that I'm extremely proud of you and what, what you did. Had to be very, very difficult and you're one hell of a kid because that had ta be the hardest thing you probably ever done in your life. And I don't even know if I could even feel what you hadda just do and I, I truly believe you're one hell of a kid.[2]

Not to be left out of the praise party, Wiegert artfully added, "And that goes for both of us. We both believe that."[3] When the multipart interrogation recommenced, so too did the positive feedback. When the interrogators wanted to add the sexual-assault angle to Dassey's story, they said, "OK Brendan, you're doing a good job. . . . Tell us more about what you heard. . . . Was a female screaming?"[4] And after going around in circles, and finally getting Dassey to say that Avery admitted to raping Halbach, they rewarded him. "Now [we] can start believing you, OK?"[5]

Similarly, when the interrogators pressed for details about what Avery and Dassey did in the garage, they made sure Dassey knew he was on the right track.

> OK Brendan, we gotta, I think, I think you're doin' a real good job up to this point of, ah, coming forward and stuff. . . . Again, we have, w-we know that some things happened in that garage, and in that car, we know that. You need to tell us about this so we know you're tellin' the truth.[6]

So Dassey tried to tell them the details they wanted. After all, they said he was "doin' a real good job," but if he didn't keep doing a good job, they wouldn't "go to bat" for him with the other government agents who wanted to prosecute him. But despite his best efforts, Dassey wasn't able to provide the *right* details. When asked whether Halbach was shot "on the garage floor" or "in the truck," he guessed wrong: "Innn the truck."[7]

Quite obviously, this was a guess rather than a lie. By this point, Dassey had already admitted to raping Halbach, helping Avery murder her, and helping him put her body in the fire. What advantage could he possibly gain from saying that Halbach was shot in her truck if, in fact, he knew she had been shot on the garage floor? The truck or the garage—who cares? It certainly made no difference from Dassey's standpoint. However, Wiegert and Fassbender cared a great deal; their theory of the case was that Halbach was shot on the garage floor. Their desire to shape the confession prompted Wiegert to say, "Ah huh, come on, now where was she shot? Be honest here."[8] Fassbender added the now-tiresome refrain: "The truth."[9]

In order to please Wiegert and Fassbender, Dassey changed his answer to the only remaining option in the two-option multiple-choice question. Halbach was shot, he now said, "In the garage."[10] He even added, parroting his interrogators' words, "She was on the, the garage floor."[11] This pleased the interrogators, who offered some more well-timed positive feedback. "She was on the garage floor, OK. That makes sense. Now we believe you."[12] And this was quite good from Dassey's perspective. As Fassbender had told him repeatedly, "I gotta believe in you" in order to "go to bat for you."[13] And the interrogators *were* believing in him.

After two days and four interrogations, Wiegert and Fassbender had just turned Dassey from Avery's witness—remember, Dassey initially reported seeing Halbach drive away from what the police believed was the scene of her murder—into the state's star witness *against* Avery. Granted, the story was so unbelievable that prosecutor Ken Kratz ultimately decided not to use it, or Dassey, at Avery's trial. But the interrogators didn't know that at the time. So even as they were taking Dassey into custody after their fourth interrogation, Wiegert continued the positive feedback. "Brendan, you did the right thing. . . . So you did the right thing here, by telling us what happened. OK."[14] To add additional insult to injury, he trotted out the honesty theme one last time. "Just remember that in the future, OK, you need to be honest."[15]

Fassbender, in perhaps the biggest lie of the entire case, then added, "Your cooperation and help with us is gonna work *in your favor*."[16] He then capped things off in businesslike fashion with a final request. Given that he believed Kratz would want Dassey to testify at Avery's trial, Fassbender told Dassey that the state would "appreciate your continued cooperation."[17]

18

"WOULD YOU LIKE A SANDWICH?"

When I first started practicing law, my mom came to court to watch one of my cases. She had arrived early and watched the previous case—a suppression hearing where the defense lawyer argued that his client's confession to the police was not voluntary and, therefore, should not be used at trial. The testimony and argument, my mom later told me, was dominated by a single issue: whether the police offered the defendant "a sandwich, snack, or beverage."

My mom thought the prosecutor and judge were either slow on the uptake or "nuts," as she put it, for dwelling on such an obviously irrelevant topic. And to an intelligent observer outside the world of criminal law, sodas and snack foods should have little to do with the admissibility of a confession. Yet, whenever the police interrogate a suspect, they magically turn into the most generous hosts on the planet; even the cops in middle Wisconsin will demonstrate an unparalleled level of southern-style hospitality.

This raises two questions. Did Wiegert and Fassbender offer Dassey a sandwich, snack, or beverage? And if so, why? The answer to the first question is yes, Wiegert and Fassbender offered Dassey more food and beverages than he could possibly consume—more on that below. The answer to the second question—Why?—is this: When the police interrogate a suspect, they not only want to get the suspect to confess, but they also want to ensure that the prosecutor will be able to use that confession at the suspect-turned-defendant's jury trial.

As discussed in chapter 12, in order to be admissible the confession must be the product of the defendant's free and voluntary choice. And as fans of *Making a Murderer* know, Wisconsin appellate courts will label just about anything as voluntary; judges simply do not want to suppress a defendant's confession under any circumstances. So a court will look for little things on which to hang its hat, thus allowing it to find that the confession was not coerced, but instead was made of the defendant's own free will.

So what do snacks and sodas have to do with that? As Dassey's state appellate court held, they go to whether the police applied "improper pressures" on Dassey.[1] If the interrogators offered him food and something to drink, that was a figurative "box" the court could "check" in favor of "no improper pressures." And once a couple of these figurative boxes on the state's side of the ledger have been checked, the court can find that the confession was voluntary—no matter how many different pressure tactics the interrogators actually used.

Dassey's state appellate court decision was incredibly brief and devoid of analysis—literally. The decision merely summarized and adopted the trial judge's findings. The appellate court spent one paragraph regurgitating a few case names, and then used two short paragraphs to dispense with Dassey's argument. And right near the beginning of those two paragraphs, the court "checked" the food and beverage "box" in favor of the state. The court wrote: Dassey "was interviewed while seated on an upholstered couch, never was physically restrained and was *offered food, beverages* and restroom breaks."[2]

This, combined with another true but irrelevant fact—that Dassey was enrolled "in mostly regular-track high school classes"—and one colossal falsehood—that Wiegert and Fassbender did *not* use "threats or promises of leniency"—was more than enough for the appellate court to agree with the trial court: "Dassey's confession was voluntary and admissible."[3]

Wiegert and Fassbender had been trained that the appellate court would later rely on their generosity with food and drink. That's why they incorporated another simple trick into their interrogation routine: they repeatedly asked Dassey if he wanted a sandwich, snack, or soda.

For example, at Mishicot High School, right after drilling Dassey about seeing arms, legs, skulls, and other body parts, Wiegert asked him, "Do you want to take a little break, get a soda? You need something to drink?"[4] Dassey declined, but because police interrogators have a difficult time taking no for an answer in any context, Fassbender pressed, "What kind? Do you want something?"[5] Similarly, after getting into more gory detail at the Two Rivers Police Department, Wiegert asked, "Are you doing OK? Do you need a soda or something?"[6]

The interrogators' generosity continued, and in fact dramatically improved, at the Manitowoc County Sheriff's Department interrogation. Even after Dassey told them he wasn't hungry, Fassbender asked, "Drink, anything, bag of chips or something, cuz this may, you know, be a little while."[7] "Naw," Dassey responded.[8] Fassbender then reinforced a classic cop stereotype: "OK, doughnut?"[9] Dassey declined that snack food as well. A short time later, Fassbender pressed, "Soda? Water? You sure?"[10]

The interrogators' generosity was ongoing. After their discussion of Halbach's rape, blood-soaked throat slashing, and murder by gunshot, Wiegert interjected, "You need a break, any soda or somethin'? OK. We can get you a soda if you want one. Would you like one?"[11] Fassbender added, "We got some food up here, sandwich or anything, you want somethin'? Are you sure?"[12] Not surprisingly, given the gory topic of discussion and the uncomfortable position he was in, Dassey responded, "Not hungry."[13] Not to be deterred, within minutes Fassbender was back at it. "Want somethin' to eat? You sure?"[14] Dassey again explained the obvious: "Ain't hungry."[15]

Wiegert, perhaps having missed some of this food-related discourse, wanted to leave nothing to chance. To make sure Dassey's culinary desires were satisfied, he asked, "Sandwich or anything?"[16] Then, after more discussion of how Dassey allegedly disposed of Halbach's blood-drenched body, Fassbender resumed the role of headwaiter. "Do you want somethin' to eat? Looks like you're a little hungry."[17] Wiegert again offered the menu's sole choice for the main course. "How about a sandwich? Should we get you a sandwich?"[18]

Offering food and beverage is such an ingrained part of Wiegert and Fassbender's routine that, much like lying to the suspect, it is probably difficult to turn off. Even after the interrogation ended, and Fassbender was watching Dassey say goodbye to his mother before being ripped away from his simple existence to be locked in a cage, he reflexively asked, "Do you want another water Brendan?"[19]

Interestingly, Wiegert and Fassbender had asked Dassey so many times whether he wanted "a soda" that Dassey actually incorporated it into the yarn he was spinning about Halbach's rape. After the interrogators insisted that Dassey must have gone inside Avery's trailer after hearing screams, he was forced to create some details on the fly. In Ken Kratz's favorite part of the confession, Dassey said that he knocked on Avery's door and was greeted by his sweaty uncle: "He's got a white shirt on with red shorts and all sweaty."[20] According to Dassey's story, he entered Avery's trailer where Halbach was tied up in the bedroom, still screaming. Avery then told Dassey that he was in the middle of sexually assaulting her.

On the edge of their seats and eager for details, Fassbender urges Dassey to "play the video [in your mind] for us Bud, tell us what's happenin'."[21] The following exchange ensues:

Brendan: He asks me in the kitchen.

Wiegert: He what?

Brendan: He walks me into the kitchen.

Fassbender: What does he say to you?

Brendan: *If I want a soda.*

Fassbender: Does he know you've heard [Halbach screaming]? Is she still sayin' stuff?

Brendan: Yeah. . . .

Wiegert: It's OK, tell us what happened. What did he say to you?

Brendan: That he never got some of that stuff [Halbach] so he wanted to get some. . . .

Fassbender: Now I can start believing you, OK?

Wiegert: So *do you have a soda?*

Brendan: Mm huh.

Wiegert: And what happens next?

Brendan: *I open the soda and I drink some.*[22]

Dassey then explains that their discussion, over "a soda," included Avery expressing his plan to continue the sexual assault, and his invitation that Dassey join in the crime.

One would think that, even for the most experienced criminals, this is not the type of thing that would be discussed casually over sodas while the victim is screaming in a nearby room. And it certainly doesn't seem like something a first time, sixteen-year-old criminal would be calm enough to do. Instead, it is far more likely that Dassey heard Wiegert and Fassbender offer him "a soda" so many times that he simply weaved it into his story to buy time while dreaming up the next detail.

In any case, even after the interrogation concluded, Wiegert and Fassbender's generosity did not end. After they told Dassey's mother that her sixteen-year-old son had just confessed to committing a violent rape and murder and was going to jail, Fassbender just couldn't stop himself. "Do you want a sandwich, Barb? We have some here."[23] Barb's response exposes the pure absurdity of Fassbender's offer. "I'd probably just throw it up anyhow."[24]

And as for the Wisconsin appellate courts' reasoning that sodas and snacks can overcome a variety of interrogation tactics—including lies, threats, promises, and repeated and grossly leading questions—to render a statement "voluntary," that's just legal fiction. Dassey's appellate lawyers explained it best: "The psychological effects of false promises of leniency cannot be cured by placing a defendant on a couch or giving him a Sprite."[25]

19

REMAINING OVERCONFIDENT

Chapter 4 demonstrated how most false confessions would not happen without the interrogator formulating a theory of the case and then refusing to modify it—evidence be damned. Then, once the interrogator locks into his predetermined view of events, he forces his set of facts onto the suspect who eventually adopts it to produce the false confession.

But just as the police have unwavering confidence before the interrogation begins, they also maintain that level of confidence during the interrogation and after it ends. In this way, the police labor under a form of the sunk-cost fallacy: they are so invested in their theory that they simply *must* maintain the faith. If they start doubting their abilities to "know" what really happened, that would mean the time they invested would be lost forever, their effort will have been wasted, and the case will remain unsolved. And nobody wants that.

But keeping the faith isn't always easy, particularly when the interrogation produces an obviously fabricated story that is contradicted by the physical evidence. For example, thanks to Wiegert and Fassbender's leading questions, Dassey described a violent, blood-soaked stabbing and throat slashing in Avery's bedroom, after which they dragged Halbach's bleeding body through the trailer and into the garage, where Avery then shot her ten times.[1] Even Wiegert had to step back and wonder—at least momentarily—about this story. During a brief reality check, he asked:

> You said that you had cut her throat. Here's the thing Brendan, when you cut somebody's throat, they bleed a lot, OK? Am I right? She'd bleed a lot, so I know you had blood on ya, it's pretty much impossible not to. Did you have blood on you? What about when you moved her?[2]

Yet Dassey had no blood on his clothing or his shoes. And despite numerous searches of Avery's trailer and garage—including searches for

93

microscopic forensic evidence conducted shortly after Halbach's remains were discovered—not a speck of Halbach's blood was found. (Yet there was ample evidence of Avery's DNA, and even blood, thus demonstrating that the trailer and garage had not been scrubbed.)

And Wiegert and Fassbender should have had additional reservations about the yarn they were helping Dassey to spin. Not only was his story contradicted by the evidence—to use Wiegert's words, his tale was "pretty much impossible"—but it was also internally inconsistent. Dassey's appellate lawyers explain:

> The officers asked Brendan to tell the story of stabbing and choking—but he couldn't keep his story straight without help. At first, Brendan said Halbach was uncuffed, tied up, stabbed, and choked, but on the second telling he said that she was stabbed and choked, then uncuffed and tied up. At several points, the interrogators had to chime in when he showed signs of not knowing what to say.[3]

But these inconsistencies are small in the grand scheme of the two-day interrogation extravaganza. At one time, Dassey had Halbach being stabbed in an entirely different location. During the Mishicot High School interrogation, he said that Avery "tied her up and stabbed her in the truck," rather than in the bedroom of his trailer.[4] And he told a similar story at the Two Rivers Police Department, where he claimed Avery "tied her up in her jeep thing and stabbed her in the stomach."[5]

These dramatic contradictions can be expected when the interrogators use threats, promises, lies, and leading questions to produce their finished product. In many ways, Dassey was merely the conduit for *their* theory, and was not recounting events he had personally witnessed. And the interrogators should have realized—and to some extent did realize—this was happening.

For example, after they insisted that the bonfire had already been started by the time Dassey arrived at Avery's trailer, Fassbender realized that this didn't make any sense after all. Confronting Dassey—as though *Dassey* was the one who had provided this piece of information—Fassbender said, "Mark and I have a little trouble understanding why he's got this big fire going if he was actually talking about putting her in the pond."[6]

Similarly, in the most famous scene of the interrogation, it was Wiegert and Fassbender who got Dassey to agree with them that Avery *shot* Halbach. But soon they realized that this didn't mesh with the other parts of the story they had created and forced on Dassey. So they asked him, "Can you tell me why, i–if Teresa was, was dead when she was in the garage, why you would shoot or, why he would shoot a dead body?"[7]

But as soon as the interrogators would have these momentary, lucid insights, they would immediately suppress their doubts and soldier on with their mission. They were simply too invested in preserving Dassey's confession and their theory of the case to let conflicting facts get in the way.

Another red flag was raised when the interrogators first pressed Dassey, at Mishicot High School, about the color of Halbach's shirt. Dassey first reported that it was a "*blue* shirt" with "some blood" on it.[8] At the Two Rivers Police Department, he reiterated that it was blue, and added that it was "a button-up shirt"[9] and had "a hole"[10] in it. By the time of the Manitowoc Sheriff's Department interrogation, however, he described Halbach's shirt as "a *white* T-shirt" that "was ripped."[11] Within minutes, he then changed it to a "*black*" shirt that was a "button up" style.[12]

Wiegert, again, had doubts. He confronted Dassey, telling him that in their earlier interrogation "you said it was blue. Do you remember what color it was? If you don't remember, say you don't remember."[13] Dassey admitted that he didn't remember. Fassbender later asked Dassey, "Now the shirt, earlier you told us the shirt had blood on it, had a hole in it, was that not true?"[14] "No," Dassey replied.[15]

The interrogators were faced with a child who described the same shirt as being three different colors, two different styles, and in two different conditions—once as having blood on it and a hole in it, and once having neither. The child then admitted that he made everything up. Yet Wiegert and Fassbender were only momentarily bothered by this—they viewed it as a minor speed bump rather than a substantial problem. They were so determined to obtain and use the confession that they didn't stop to think, "Hey, maybe none of this makes any sense, and maybe the story keeps changing because this kid is just saying things to make us happy and not because they're true."

But instead of having this moment of calm, rational reflection, Wiegert and Fassbender moved forward with their mission—creating, and then promptly ignoring, more red flags in the process. The end product of their single-minded determination, unsurprisingly, was a nonsensical mess. As false confession expert Lawrence T. White wrote in 2007 regarding Dassey's statements:

> Brendan is a vulnerable individual due to his low intelligence, poor memory skills, and passive demeanor. The police repeatedly pressured Brendan to provide them with details that conformed to their theory of the crime. Brendan's statements were often inconsistent, ambivalent, and self-contradictory. In sum, there are *many reasons to question the trustworthiness and voluntariness* of Brendan Dassey's so-called "confession."[16]

Wiegert and Fassbender ignored these "many reasons to question the trustworthiness" of Dassey's story and instead "reassured Brendan *five* times on February 27 and *thirty-one* times on March 1 that they 'already knew' what he had done."[17] So even assuming that Wiegert and Fassbender were open to new evidence before the interrogations began, once they told Dassey a total of thirty-six times that they "already knew" the truth, even *they* had come to believe their own spin.

The interrogators' unwavering, but unwarranted, belief in what happened was obvious at the end of their fourth interrogation when they broke the news to Dassey's mother, Barb, that her child had confessed to rape and murder. Even Barb knew that something wasn't right. She asked the interrogators, "Were you pressuring him?"[18] It's hard to know, at this point, whether Wiegert was just playing dumb when he responded, "Who are you talking about?"[19] When Dassey's mother stated the obvious—that she was referring to her son—Wiegert continued: "What do you mean, pressuring him?"[20] (Could he really have been that clueless, or was his response just more of the same cop-style gamesmanship?)

Wiegert then gave a short monologue that captures the essence of this chapter and nicely illustrates the interrogators' overconfidence in their abilities. "No, we told him we needed to know the truth. We've been doing this job a long time Barb and we can tell when people aren't telling the truth."[21]

As for Dassey, he was going to jail. Despite the interrogators' multiple promises, "the truth" did not set him free.

PULLING THE RUG FROM UNDER

Wiegert and Fassbender's promises of leniency, which were conditioned upon Dassey telling them what they wanted to hear, were reinforced by the interrogators' repeated "assurances that they 'already knew' everything Brendan had supposedly done."[1] These assurances, in turn, "indicated that nothing Brendan said could shock them into reneging on their promises—giving him *carte blanche* to say the worst things he could think of" as he tried to satisfy his interrogators.[2] "There can be no doubt that Brendan thought he had been offered a virtual get-out-of-jail-free card."[3]

And Dassey tried to use his card after he agreed that he had committed three very serious crimes—including the murder of Teresa Halbach. He would have confessed to anything the interrogators asked of him, but these crimes were more than enough—even for Wiegert and Fassbender. And now that Dassey had performed his side of the bargain, it was time for the interrogators to hold up their end of the deal. Near the end of their fourth interrogation, their exchange went as follows:

Brendan: How long is this gonna take?

Wiegert: It shouldn't take a whole lot longer.

Brendan: Do you think I can get [back to school] before one twenty-nine?

Wiegert: Um, probably not.

Brendan: Oh.

Wiegert: What's at one twenty-nine?

Brendan: Well, I have a project due in sixth hour.

Wiegert: OK. Well, we'll worry about that later, OK?[4]

Even though Dassey gave them the confession they relentlessly demanded, the interrogators weren't taking him back to school and, in fact, Fassbender was far from done. He needed to tie up a few loose ends of the story they had fed to Dassey. "We think you're doin' pretty good so far but there's some areas that we have ta revisit, OK, and then some other questions."[5] And he couldn't help but trot out their tired mantra about how they already know the truth, and how Dassey should just agree with them. "And, and again, don't make us work so hard for this . . . just get the truth out right away, cuz again we, we have a pretty good knowledge of what happened there."[6]

As they had done throughout the interrogation, they would ask a question, Dassey would give an answer they didn't like, and they insisted on truth and honesty. Then Dassey would say exactly what they had asked him to say, but the interrogators would realize that their story really didn't make sense after all. So they would scold Dassey as if *he*, rather than *they*, had provided the details that suddenly displeased them. Their final bit of nonsensical, wheel-spinning dialogue included the following exchange:

Fassbender: What happened to Teresa's other personal effects? I mean, ah, a woman usually has a purse, right? Tell us what happened ta that?

Brendan: I don't know what happened to it.

Fassbender: What happened ta her, ah, her cell phone? Don't try ta, ta think of somethin' just—

Brendan: I don't know. . . .

Fassbender: Did Steven tell ya what he did with those things?

Brendan: No.

Fassbender: I need ya to tell us the truth.

Brendan: Yeah.

Fassbender: What did he do with her her possessions?

Brendan: I don't know.[7]

Brendan clearly said he didn't know—*four* times. And Fassbender even paid lip service to the idea that Dassey shouldn't just make up an answer if he didn't know. But just like the person who says, "Don't get me anything for my birthday," but then expects a present, Fassbender kept pressing and pressing for the answer he claimed not to want. And then Wiegert jumped into the mix with the now-familiar demand of honesty, and the two interrogators got their prize—sort of.

> Wiegert: Brendan . . . It's really important that you continue being honest with us. OK, don't start lying now. The hard part's over. Do you know what happened ta those items?
>
> Brendan: He burnt 'em.
>
> Wiegert: How do you know?
>
> Brendan: Because when I passed it there was like, like a purse in there and stuff. . . .
>
> Wiegert: What else was in there?
>
> Brendan: Like garbage bags, some. . . .
>
> Wiegert: Tell me what you saw in there exactly.
>
> Brendan: Like they were buried underneath ah, garbage, a garbage bag that was—
>
> Wiegert: How do you know, or *how could you see them if they were underneath a garbage bag?*[8]

Good question, Mark.

Eventually, however, the interrogators had to wrap things up—all good things, as they say, must end. It was now time to let Dassey know that they had not been acting as his father, and they were not going to stand behind him. And they never had any intention of going to bat for him; instead, they had bad intentions from the get-go. Fassbender broke the news to Dassey this way:

> You know obviously that we're police officers. OK. And because of what you told us, we're gonna have ta arrest you. Did you kinda figure that was coming? For, for what you did we, we can't let you go right now. The law will not let us. And you're not gonna be able to go home tonight. All right? . . . Did you kinda, and be, honestly, the, after telling us what you told us, you kinda figured this was coming? Yeah?[9]

One has to wonder how Wiegert and Fassbender felt about yanking the rug from under the stunned child—a child who, at their urging, trusted them and believed they were looking out for his interests. Based on the interrogators' behavior up to this point, one can't help but think that, at least on some level, they might have enjoyed lowering the boom on the kid.

Put another way, they had repeatedly tricked, psychologically manipulated, and blatantly lied to the child. And they did all of this, apparently, without any misgivings. From there, it is not a big leap to think they may have gotten a charge out of telling Dassey that he had been duped. Sure, they were two grown men and Dassey was a sixteen-year-old kid with learning disabilities. And, admittedly, they needed four cracks at him to get what they wanted. But a win is still a win. To use an analogy, it's probably at least a little fun for a professional tennis player to hit an ace against a movie star in a charity tennis match. An ace is still an ace.

But if Wiegert and Fassbender did enjoy it, they were careful not to rub Dassey's face in their triumph. Not only did they think they would need him to testify against Avery down the road, but they also wanted more out of him that very day. So, rather than doing a victory dance, Fassbender kept the lies and promises flowing:

> Your cooperation and help with us is gonna work in your favor. I can't say what it's gonna do or where your gonna end up but its gonna work in your favor and we appreciate your continued cooperation . . . going out to the house and going in the house and gettin' a few items, and about you going there with us and . . . um pointing out those areas that we wanted ya to point out. Is that all right? . . . Do you know where those shoes are that you were wearing that day? The red shoes? . . . What about the jacket?[10]

But as bad as this was for Dassey, it wasn't the biggest rug-yanking he would experience in this case. Sure, the cops said they were on his side when they were really working against him. But an even bigger surprise would await him when he met his attorney, Len Kachinsky, who really was—at least legally speaking—on Dassey's side. Their bizarre relationship will be the subject of chapter 22. But first, the next chapter moves us out of the interrogation room and into trial-preparation mode. It's time for Ken Kratz to take Dassey's "confession" to the media. Warning: things are about to get "sweaty."

Part IV
TRIALS, TRIBULATIONS, AND APPEALS

21

POISONING THE JURY POOL

Once Wiegert and Fassbender extracted a confession from Dassey, prosecutor Ken Kratz and his team had to think about how to present that piece of evidence at Dassey's jury trial. The presentation was going to be incredibly important, as the state didn't have an eyewitness or any physical evidence linking Dassey to the crimes.

Just as the interrogators have tactics to get confessions, prosecutors have tactics to win jury trials. One of their tricks is to start "trying the case" to the potential jurors, before trial, during the jury selection process known as *voir dire*. This allows the prosecutor to start indoctrinating the jurors early, thus increasing the odds of a conviction. But if early is better, why not start even sooner than that? Why not try the case in the media, long before the would-be jurors are even assembled in the courthouse? If the prosecutor can convince the general public of Dassey's guilt, and if the eventual jurors will be drawn from the general public, then the state can win its case before anyone steps foot into the courtroom.

Fortunately for Dassey, there is a rule that prohibits this tactic. Wisconsin Supreme Court Rule (SCR) 20:3.6 is an ethics rule governing attorney conduct and pretrial publicity. It states, "A lawyer . . . shall not make an extrajudicial statement that . . . will be disseminated by means of public communication and will have a substantial likelihood of materially prejudicing an adjudicative proceeding in the matter."[1] More specifically, "in a criminal case," it is an ethics violation to tell the media about *the existence or contents of any confession*, admission, or statement given *by a defendant or suspect*."[2]

Yet, despite this rule that seems to prohibit telling the media about a defendant's alleged confession, that's exactly what the prosecutorial team did. On March 2, 2006, less than twenty-four hours after Wiegert and Fassbender finally dragged something resembling a confession out of Dassey, Kratz was singing loudly and proudly to the media. By racing into a press conference before the ink was even dry on the interrogators' written reports, Kratz likely had only a limited opportunity to read, let alone carefully study, Dassey's so-called confession. Nonetheless, Kratz rendered the following dramatic reading, complete with novelistic flair and several well-timed pauses:

> We have now determined what occurred. . . . Sixteen-year-old Brendan Dassey, who lives next door to Steven Avery in a trailer, returned home on the bus from school. . . . He retrieved the mail and noticed one of the letters was for his uncle, Steven Avery. As Brendan approaches the trailer, as he actually gets several hundred feet away from the trailer, a long, long way from the trailer, Brendan already starts to hear the screams. As Brendan approaches the trailer, he hears louder screams for help, recognizes it to be of a female individual, and he knocks on Steven Avery's trailer door.[3]

Then comes the often-mocked part of the presser, where Kratz eerily uses the word "sweat," or a variation thereof, two too many times.

> [T]he person he knows as his uncle, who is partially dressed, who is *full of sweat*, opens the door and greats his sixteen-year-old nephew. Brendan accompanies his *sweaty*, forty-three-year-old uncle down the hallway to Steven Avery's bedroom. And there they find Teresa Halbach, completely naked, and shackled to the bed. Teresa Halbach is begging Brendan for her life. The evidence that we've uncovered establishes that . . . during the rape, Teresa's begging for help . . . Brendan, under the instruction of Steven Avery, cuts Teresa Halbach's throat, but she still doesn't die.[4]

Of course, the "evidence that we've uncovered" was nothing more than the statement the interrogators fed to, and then extracted from, Brendan Dassey in their four interrogations over forty-eight hours. Nonetheless, Kratz went on to discuss the choking and stomach stabbing, followed by details about how they dragged the bloody mess of a body outside, where they repeatedly shot her and then burned the corpse. (Never mind that the physical evidence contradicted this wild tale.)

How could Kratz do this? SCR 20:3.6 clearly prohibits disclosing "the existence or contents of any confession . . . given by a defendant or suspect." In criminal law, however, whenever there's a rule that a prosecutor is supposed to follow, there's a way around that rule. And in this case, there are at least two ways.

First, SCR 20:3.6 goes on to say that, notwithstanding the prohibition on disclosing confessions to the media, a prosecutor may disclose "information contained in a public record."[5] Therefore, once a secretary or legal assistant in the prosecutor's office typed Dassey's confession into his criminal complaint and filed it, the confession became part of "a public record." And, as Kratz argued when litigating Steven Avery's case, he is allowed to disclose information contained in such a record.[6] This simple administrative act of copying and pasting appears to obliterate the rule against disclosing the "contents of any confession." Some would argue, however, that it simply can't be that easy to destroy an ethics rule; if it is, then what's the point of having the rule in the first place?

But in that case, SCR 20:30.6 also provides Kratz with a second exception. It goes on to state that a prosecutor

> may make a statement that a reasonable lawyer would believe is required to protect a client from the substantial likelihood of undue prejudicial effect of recent publicity not initiated by the lawyer or the lawyer's client. A statement made pursuant to this paragraph shall be limited to such information as is necessary to mitigate the recent adverse publicity.[7]

And as Kratz also argued when litigating Avery's case, "Steven Avery, family members, supporters, and other citizens advanced the theory that Avery was being 'set up' by law enforcement officials."[8] Therefore, Kratz's presser was meant to protect the state from such adverse publicity.

But even assuming that Kratz's disclosure of Dassey's confession was truly intended to counter the conspiracy theorists, this still raises several questions. Did the conspiracy theorists really create a "substantial likelihood" of undue prejudice to the state? Would a "reasonable lawyer" believe that an over-the-top, novelistic reading of Dassey's confession was "required" to protect the state? Wasn't the state the party that "initiated" the back-and-forth when it made its first statement to the media accusing Avery of murder? And was Kratz's dramatic rendering of Dassey's alleged confession—complete with multiple references to "sweat"—reasonably "limited" to what was "necessary to mitigate" the conspiracy theorists' message?

Even if Kratz's disclosure of the confession could somehow pass all of those tests—and, in fairness, Kratz's conduct in this regard was not found to have violated any ethics rule—what about *Dassey's* right to a fair trial with an impartial jury? After all, it is *his* supposed confession. Yet all of the justifications for disclosing it to the media were based on Steven Avery and his conspiracy-theorist supporters. Dassey never made any statements to the media that would cause undue prejudice for the state to mitigate, yet *he* has to suffer the negative impact of Kratz's pretrial media blitz, including the dramatic reading of the confession.

But did Dassey really suffer from Kratz trying the case in the media? Surely, the media must have questioned Kratz about the circumstances under which Dassey's alleged confession was obtained. Someone must have asked, for example, whether an adult was present when Dassey talked, whether it was the interrogators or Dassey who came up with the details, whether the statement was consistent with the known physical evidence, and whether the interrogators made any promises or threats to extract the confession. Someone must have asked these questions—didn't they?

Unfortunately, the media showed little interest in this level of detail. And worse yet, many members of the media simply jumped to the most sensationalistic conclusion possible. In a presentation even more dramatic then Kratz's press conference, one newscast stated that the picture of Halbach's rape and murder was "painted by a sixteen-year-old boy who couldn't keep his terrible secret any longer."[9] Of course, the exact opposite was true: Wiegert and Fassbender fed Dassey the details and then painfully extracted those same facts over the course of four interrogations. The confession was not, as the media portrayed, the result of Dassey unburdening his soul.

Similarly, another newscast stated that the interrogators "used his statements like instructions to put together pieces of a sick puzzle."[10] Once again, the opposite was true: Wiegert and Fassbender had already "put together pieces of [the] sick puzzle" in their heads. Then, based on what they believed must have happened, they created the details to support their preexisting theory of the crime.

And the media's accounts resonated with the Wisconsin citizens who comprised Dassey's jury pool. Many were all too eager to accept, and even internalize, the state's story. For example, at Kratz's March 2 press conference he stated that Steven Avery "*invites* his sixteen-year-old nephew to sexually assault this woman,"[11] and that Dassey, "*under the instruction* of Steven Avery, cuts Teresa Halbach's throat."[12] After hearing this theory, one citizen interviewed by the media said of Dassey, "I think he did help him out. I don't think he was the master behind it, but I think he helped him out."[13]

The citizen expressed this conclusion with great certainty, as if he had personally investigated the facts and formulated an independent and informed opinion. The far more likely explanation, of course, is that he simply heard Kratz's account that Avery invited and instructed Dassey to commit the crime, and then internalized the story as if it were his own original thought. This, of course, is exactly what prosecutors want. If the would-be jurors are convinced of guilt before stepping into the courthouse, the battle is won before it is even fought.

This example nicely illustrates the dangers of a prosecutor disclosing a defendant's alleged confession to the media. Of course, SCR 20:3.6 initially pretends to prohibit such disclosure to protect defendants from these dangers. But by the end of the lengthy, multipart, exception-riddled rule, there are so many holes through which a prosecutor can crawl that the rule—like many other attorney ethics rules—may as well not even exist.[14]

But despite the "sweaty," pro-state spin that Kratz put on the confession—to the delight of the media and for the entertainment of the news-consuming public—the prosecutorial team knew it had problems with its single, unsupported, and even contradicted piece of evidence. Earlier chapters demonstrated that, during the interrogation, even Wiegert and Fassbender had their doubts; on several occasions they told Dassey that the yarn he was spinning just didn't make any sense and, in some parts, was even "impossible." But Kratz and his cohorts were about to catch a big break. Enter defense attorney Len Kachinsky.

22

SPIT SHINING THE EVIDENCE

As the last chapter explained, Ken Kratz's pretrial media tour went a long way toward winning the case before it even started. But the state's real break came when Len Kachinsky was appointed as Dassey's defense lawyer.

When defending a criminal case, there is a general rule that selecting a defense strategy is the lawyer's decision, not the client's. And this makes sense, as the lawyer is supposedly trained to make that choice. However, there are at least two exceptions to this rule. First, any strategy that involves the client pleading guilty requires the client's approval. The reason is that, by law, only the client can make this particular decision.[1] And second, even when the attorney's defense strategy does not involve the client pleading to some charge, the attorney cannot decide on a strategy until he or she has adequately investigated the case and met with the client.[2]

Despite these two limitations, Kachinsky decided—before reviewing the case and even before talking with his client—that his defense strategy was for Dassey to plead guilty and, hopefully, get a reduced sentence. Dassey's appellate lawyers argued:

> [Kachinsky's] earliest remarks to the media foreshadowed this plan; on the same day he was appointed, for instance, he told the press that Brendan was "morally and legally responsible." Kachinsky made this remark, which he later conceded was an admission of Brendan's guilt, *before he had even met his client or discussed his plea idea with him.*[3]

Telling the world that a defendant is "morally and legally responsible" accomplishes several things; however, none of them are good for the defendant. Most notably, this public concession of guilt corroborated Kratz's media blitz. And Kachinsky's own media tour, like Kratz's, was ongoing. As another example, Kachinsky told the press that the interrogators were *not* "putting words" in Dassey's mouth,[4] and that Dassey "was remorseful" and "there was no defense."[5]

It didn't matter to Kachinsky that, when he eventually met with his client, Dassey insisted he was innocent and had falsely confessed. Much like the government interrogators who ignored any piece of evidence that contradicted their theory of the case, Kachinsky was firmly locked into his defense strategy of Dassey pleading guilty and cooperating with the state. And by carrying out this strategy, Kachinsky was polishing up the state's only piece of evidence: the confession.

Kachinsky then did something that is probably unprecedented in the history of criminal law: he hired a private investigator, Michael O'Kelly, to interrogate Dassey again. Kachinsky's goal was to obtain a confession from his own client that the state could use to corroborate, and therefore strengthen, Dassey's earlier confession to Wiegert and Fassbender. This would, presumably, please the prosecutor, who then, hopefully, would recommend a reduced sentence when Dassey eventually entered his guilty plea.

O'Kelly began interrogating Dassey the same way the government's interrogators did: he refused to accept any claims of innocence. "When Brendan told O'Kelly that he was innocent and explained that on March 1 he had been merely 'guessing' and agreeing to 'whatever [the police] said,' O'Kelly refused to listen."[6] O'Kelly then employed Wiegert and Fassbender's tactic of offering to help in exchange for Dassey telling the truth. However, much like the government's interrogators, O'Kelly equated "the truth" with whatever confirmed his preexisting beliefs.

> [O'Kelly] promised that if Brendan confessed again, then "I'll help you through this process and you will not be doing life in prison." . . . If Brendan denied involvement, on the other hand, O'Kelly told him that his defense team would do nothing to help him escape a frightening fate: "[I]f you lie to me, guess what I have to do? I have to stand up, put everything away, and leave. Because that means that you want to go to prison for the rest of your life." . . . Under O'Kelly's watchful eye, he gradually wrote out a full confession.[7]

By this point, then, things were really starting to look up for the state. Sure, it initially had serious problems with the muddled, garbage confession that Wiegert and Fassbender eventually pulled out of Dassey. But Kratz was able to mitigate those problems through his press conferences, and Kachinsky helped the state immensely by launching his own media tour. Then Kachinsky got Dassey to confess to O'Kelly, and he promptly delivered the confession to Wiegert and Fassbender on a platter.

But then Kachinsky, Wiegert, and Fassbender—all of whom wanted to spit shine Dassey's original confession—went too far for their own good. First, Kachinsky offered the government the chance to interrogate Dassey again. (This would be Dassey's fifth interrogation by Wiegert and Fassbender, and at least his seventh overall, including the one by O'Kelly.) And second, the two government agents couldn't leave well enough alone; they couldn't resist the chance to have one more shot at the kid.

Dassey, now charged with several crimes including murder, was sitting in jail. So Wiegert and Fassbender interrogated him in custody, without Kachinsky present but with his permission. Their fifth interrogation was, in many ways, a repeat of their first four. Fassbender led with the same disingenuous rapport building. "I heard you were gonna watch a movie last night. What movie did ya watch?"[8] Then he and Wiegert employed the same wordplay about truth and honesty. "You've gotta be honest with us here Brendan, OK? This is your opportunity to be honest with us."[9]

Admittedly, the interrogators did add a new twist to their routine for this fifth go-around; however, they may have stolen this new tactic from O'Kelly, who proved to be their superior in the interrogation room. Wiegert and Fassbender convinced Dassey they were doing *him* a favor by grilling him for a fifth time. "I look at it this way, we're giving you another opportunity, we didn't need to come back here. I-if we sit here and we feel that you're not being honest with us, *we could just leave*."[10] (By comparison, O'Kelly had threatened Dassey that he would "stand up, put everything away, *and leave*.")

The two government interrogators then reverted to their tiresome tactics, including their seemingly endless claims that they already knew what happened. "Come on, Brendan. What's he telling her at this time? We know there's some talking going on, OK. We know that."[11] They also retold their most common lie: that Dassey could help himself by talking. "You need to help yourself. And that's by tellin', that's by tellin' the truth."[12] And even though they were now interrogating Dassey in the jail, Fassbender's generosity with the beverages continued. "Can I get ya a soda or water or something? . . . You sure? . . . You sure I can't get ya something, huh?"[13]

But when the dynamic duo finally got to the actual interrogation, things immediately blew up in their faces. Dassey's confession only became more garbled, confused, contradictory, and nonsensical. Putting lipstick on a pig might leave you with a slightly more attractive pig, but when you put *too much* lipstick on a pig—this was, after all, their fifth interrogation—you just get a really messy, uglier pig.

For example, in Dassey's newest version of the rape and murder, he *didn't* go to Avery's with a piece of mail; rather Avery called him and invited him over.[14] And no longer did Avery stab Halbach in the bedroom; now, both he and Dassey stabbed her, and they did so in the garage.[15] And after the stabbing, Avery shot Halbach five times, not ten.[16] Most significantly, instead of seeing Halbach's vehicle in Avery's garage or even parked outside the trailer, Dassey now admitted that he never saw it at all that day.[17] This was disastrous, so the interrogators demanded he revert to the old version of the story. "You *can't say* you didn't see the truck or know where the truck was because she had ta be in that truck after she was bleeding. OK? *That's just the way it is.*"[18] Dassey complied, and agreed with them that Halbach's truck was "backed in ta the garage."[19]

Nearly every imaginable detail of the crime had changed in this newest iteration of the confession. Before, Dassey slashed Halbach's throat in the bedroom; now, he didn't slash it at all.[20] Before, Dassey and Avery both carried Halbach out of the bedroom and Avery then went back for his rifle; this time, Avery grabbed his rifle and single-handedly carried it and Halbach to the garage, while Dassey trailed behind and carried only her clothing.[21]

Wiegert soon came to regret ever starting this fifth interrogation. "You told us last time *you* helped carry her out of the bedroom. Remember that? . . . OK, what's the truth?"[22] When Dassey said that this newest version was the truth, Fassbender had to jump in. "So you want us to believe that he carried a body and a gun, at the same time, out into the garage. . . . Ain't that nearly impossible to do unless you gave [him] the gun and then you [helped with] the body?"[23]

This wasn't the first time, and wouldn't be the last time, that the interrogators used the word "impossible" to describe Dassey's confession. And now, even the details about Halbach were in flux. Dassey previously reported that she had pubic hair, but, having forgotten what he said, was now reporting that she did not.[24] Similarly, he previously described Halbach's breasts, but now admits he never saw her breasts and, further, never touched them.[25] Even Fassbender realized this wasn't possible: "you [had] sex with her . . . *but you didn't touch her breasts?*"[26]

This fifth interrogation devolved into pure chaos. As a final example, when the interrogators previously asked Dassey what Avery had done "to her head," one of his guesses was that he had cut off her hair. This resonated with Wiegert and Fassbender—they had probably seen movies where the perpetrator took some of the victim's hair as a trophy of sorts. Hoping to find the hair—something that would actually corroborate, rather than contradict, Dassey's story—they raised the subject again.

> Fassbender: The first time we talked to you or the second time you talked about cutting her hair off. Where did the hair go? Did you cut her hair off?
>
> Brendan: Yeah.
>
> Fassbender: Where did that happen?
>
> Brendan: In the, in the bedroom.
>
> Fassbender: What ya cut the hair off with?
>
> Brendan: The knife.
>
> Fassbender: The knife you guys found in the garage? . . . *It's impossible.* You took her out to the garage and that's when you got the knife. Explain how that can be. Did you cut her hair off?
>
> Brendan: No.
>
> Fassbender: Then why did you just tell us you did? Brendan?
>
> Brendan: I don't know.[27]

Wiegert and Fassbender liked baseball analogies, so to put this in terms they could appreciate, this line of questioning was another swing-and-a-miss. In fact, the two had witnessed the government's case against Dassey go from bad (after their fourth interrogation) to good (thanks to Kratz's media tour) to great (thanks to Kachinsky's media tour and unique defense strategy). But now they had gone straight back to bad. In fact, thanks to their outrageous greed in conducting this fifth interrogation, they may have even hit a new low: disastrous.

113

However, Wiegert and Fassbender hatched a scheme to snatch victory from the jaws of justice. They devised a plan to reverse their downward trend and put an amazing gloss on their sole piece of evidence. This plan—assuming they could get the now-imprisoned child to fall for it—would overcome all of their previous coercion, all of the confession's inconsistencies, and even all of the contradictory physical evidence. They just had to convince Dassey to make one, simple phone call.

Photo 1. Avery Road. The famous (or infamous) Avery Road sign is set against a bleak winter sky in Manitowoc, Wisconsin. Teresa Halbach's remains were found nearby on the Avery property and, despite numerous holes in the government's case, the jury convicted Steven Avery of the murder. However, a great deal of evidence—including testimony and physical evidence from Avery's trial, along with new evidence developed since his conviction—indicates that a third party or parties may have committed the crime and then successfully framed Avery. Brendan Dassey was convicted in a separate trial as a party to Avery's crime. However, Dassey's conviction was based entirely on his own statements; there was no physical evidence, eyewitness, or accusation that linked him to the murder.

Photo by Rebecca Slye

Photo 2. Manitowoc County Sheriff's Department. At the time of Teresa Halbach's disappearance, the Manitowoc County Sheriff's Department was on the defensive. Steven Avery had filed a civil lawsuit for the department's role in his wrongful conviction in the 1980s, and his lawyers were in the process of deposing several of the department's agents. Yet, despite what appeared to be a conflict of interest due to the civil lawsuit, the department played a key role in developing the evidence against Avery for Halbach's murder. The sheriff's department was also the scene of Wiegert and Fassbender's fateful March 1, 2006 interrogation of Brendan Dassey. When driving Dassey from school to the department, Wiegert told him: "who knows, maybe we'll get you back as soon as we can." Instead, Dassey was interrogated and arrested.

Photo by Brenda VanCuick

Photo 3. Lawrence T. White, PhD Social psychologist and Beloit College professor Lawrence White evaluated the multiple police interrogations of Brendan Dassey. In 2007 he wrote: "The police repeatedly pressured Brendan to provide them with details that conformed to their theory of the crime. . . . [T]here are many reasons to question the trustworthiness and voluntariness of Brendan Dassey's so-called confession." Several years later, as shown in episode three of Making a Murderer, Dr. White explained: "[W]hen they say to Brendan 'be honest,' what they sort of mean is 'don't tell us that, tell us something else'—something that fits their theory of the crime."

Photo by Liisi Rannast-Kask

117

Photo 4. Manitowoc County Courthouse. Brendan Dassey was tried at the Manitowoc County Courthouse, pictured above with the Manitowoc County Jail in the background. After Dassey was convicted, Jerome L. Fox—the circuit court judge who presided over the trial—denied his post-conviction motions. Judge Fox found that Dassey had freely and voluntarily confessed (thereby rendering his confession admissible at trial). The judge also found that Dassey's trial attorneys were not "ineffective" for failing to call an expert witness, like Lawrence White, to educate the jury about coercive interrogation tactics and their link to false confessions.

Photo by Matthew Murray

Photo 5. Supreme Court of Wisconsin. Brendan Dassey's lawyers appealed the trial court's rulings to the state appellate court, arguing, in part, that Dassey's confession was coerced and its use at trial violated his constitutional rights. The court dispensed with the issue in two short paragraphs, reaching the inexplicable conclusion that Wiegert and Fassbender never made any "threats or promises of leniency." Not surprisingly, the Supreme Court of Wisconsin—located in the State Capitol Building in Madison, pictured above—refused to even hear Dassey's case. Steven Drizin, one of Dassey's appellate lawyers, explained it this way: "It would be very difficult for Brendan to get relief in the Wisconsin state court system. This case was just too much of a heater."

Photo by Michael Cicchini

Photo 6. United States District Court. Brendan Dassey's case is one of the relatively few state cases to reach the federal court system. Dassey's appellate lawyers filed a petition for writ of habeas corpus, and the United States District Court for the Eastern District of Wisconsin—located in the Federal Building in Milwaukee, pictured above—granted the writ. The Court ordered the state to release Dassey or retry him without the benefit of his so-called confession. Judge William E. Duffin wrote that Wiegert and Fassbender's "repeated false promises, when considered in conjunction with all relevant factors . . . rendered Dassey's confession involuntary." The state appealed, and a three-judge panel of the Seventh Circuit Court of Appeals agreed with Duffin. However, a seven-judge panel of the court (with two judges not participating) later disagreed. In a 4-3 decision, the flip-flopping Seventh Circuit reversed Duffin and ordered him to dismiss Dassey's petition. Dassey remains in custody with the Supreme Court of the United States being his last hope.

Photo by Michael Cicchini

23

A SIMPLE PLAN

Wiegert and Fassbender found their team—the state—down a few runs, late in the game, due to their recent error. They were too greedy in going after Dassey a fifth time, and they had muddied the waters beyond belief. In addition to all of the inconsistencies between interrogations, now Dassey couldn't even keep a story straight within an interrogation. For example, in the span of only a few transcribed pages, Wiegert extracted three different answers as to why Avery and Dassey committed the crimes.

Wiegert: OK. And what did you guys plan to do, what was your plan? Brendan talk to me, er, what was your plan?

Brendan: We did it because Steven wanted to go back to jail.

Wiegert: Did he tell you he wanted to go back to jail?

Brendan: Yeah. Cuz he missed it.

Wiegert: He didn't tell you that. Did he? Did he tell you that yes or no?[1]

This was an obvious cue that Wiegert did not like the answer Dassey had just given him. And he had good reason not to like it: it was unbelievable. What man about to receive a financial settlement for a wrongful conviction and eighteen-year incarceration—as Avery was—would want to go back to jail? So when Wiegert asked the same question a second time, just a few seconds later, Dassey changed his answer to please his interrogator.

Wiegert: And what did he say he was going to do?

Brendan: That he was gonna to kill her.

Wiegert: Did he say why?

Brendan: No.[2]

121

Obviously, Wiegert preferred some answer to no answer, so he simply asked the question a third time.

Wiegert: Well what did he tell you? Did he tell you anything? Yes or no.

Brendan: No.

Wiegert: He just said he wanted to kill her?

Brendan: Well just that he was pissed off because Jodi wasn't with him anymore.

Wiegert: OK. So he was pissed off that Jodi wasn't with him anymore so then he was gonna kill Teresa.[3]

Wiegert wasn't too satisfied with this answer either, so a while later he asked Dassey the same question a fourth time. When he got the same response, he realized that he might be able to run with it and, with some embellishment of his own, create a viable motive for Avery's crime.

Wiegert: Did he laugh about it or what? Why did, why did he say he was gonna kill her?

Brendan: Cuz he was pissed off that Jodi was in jail again.

Wiegert: Why is he pissed off that Jodi was in jail? Did he tell ya why?

Brendan: No.

Wiegert: Oh, yes he did. He told you why he was pissed off. *Probably cuz he wasn't gettin' any or something like—that's my guess.* You know what I mean by that?

Brendan: Yeah.

Wiegert: OK. Did he say that? If he didn't tell me no. But did he say that? Did he make reference ta that?

Brendan: Yeah.[4]

It was right at the end of this line of questioning—when Dassey was struggling to recount Avery's explanation of his motive—that Fassbender had enough and expressed his frustration.

You gotta forget about everything, all these people telling you what happened, what to say, what not to say. Put all those out of your head and just tell us the truth. . . . Do you know what a fact is? Brendan? . . .

A fact is something that's true. That's something that really happened. And sometimes it can get difficult to sort between the facts and everything else that people have been telling you and stories that maybe you wanted to make up because it was a, a horrible thing that happened.[5]

Fassbender's lecture was off base. First, Dassey was confused because of what Wiegert and Fassbender were repeatedly drilling into him, not because of what "these people" had said to him. Second, Dassey was making up stories because the interrogators kept asking the same questions and demanding different answers, not because of "a horrible thing that happened." And finally, it was the interrogators that destroyed the meaning of the word "truth." And while Fassbender was wise to replace the word "truth" with "fact," it made no sense to define the new word (fact) by reference to the word he was trying to replace (truth). His declaration that "a fact is something that's true" simply had no meaning given the way he and Wiegert had previously redefined the word "truth."

In any case, Wiegert and Fassbender were smart enough to realize they were in deep trouble. And just like a batter whose team is down late in the game, they had to swing for the fences. No doubt realizing that he and Fassbender (at Kachinsky's invitation) had created a whole new set of problems with their fifth interrogation, Wiegert urged Dassey to confess again—but this time to his mother. And of course, this confession must be done on the phone, rather than during her jail visit, he insists. Why? So the state can record it and play it for the jury. This would be "clean" evidence; a phone call with his mother would appear to a jury to be untainted by the interrogators' threats, false promises, leading questions, deception, manipulation, and other tactics that are known to produce false confessions.

Wiegert: OK. When you gonna tell your mom about this?

Brendan: Probably the next time I see her.

Wiegert: Cuz you've lied to her so far, right? Don't you think you should call her and tell her?

Brendan: Yeah. . . . I'm seeing her *tomorrow*. . . .

Wiegert: Then maybe it be a good idea to call her and tell her . . . *tonight*. That's what I would do. Cuz, otherwise, she's gonna be really mad here tomorrow. *Better on the phone, isn't it?*[26]

Wiegert told Dassey this was "just a suggestion."[7] But soon he upgraded his advice from "a suggestion" to a threat. "You lied one too many times to me. Sorry, we're done. . . . Do you have anything else you want to say before we leave? *I hope you call your mom before I do.*"[8]

Of course, they had no intention of actually leaving Dassey alone. Contrary to their previous lie, they were there for their own benefit, not his. So later in the interrogation—after Wiegert's empty threat that "we're done"—the interrogators again reminded Dassey to call his mother "tonight," instead of waiting for her to come visit him tomorrow. And as Fassbender's bizarre, disconnected lead-in proves, when targeting an overmatched child, even the wildest swings will sometimes connect with the pitch.

> Fassbender: Mark mentioned talkin' to your mom about this and being truthful with her now. OK? If you're truly sorry to the Halbachs, you'll be, you'll tell your mother the truth about this. OK?
>
> Wiegert: Are you gonna do that?
>
> Brendan: Yeah.
>
> Wiegert: When you gonna do that?
>
> Brendan: Tonight.[9]

The interrogators' scheme worked. "After the police allowed him to return to his cell, Brendan did as he was told. Later that day, he called his mother and tearfully told her over the recorded prison telephones that Steven had made him do 'some of it.'"[10] And this phone call with his mother was used repeatedly, and to great effect, by the prosecutors at Dassey's trial. It was used "during cross-examination of Brendan himself, during cross-examination of Brendan's expert witness, and during closing argument as a means of neutralizing Brendan's alibi."[11]

It was tough enough to explain to the jury that Dassey had falsely confessed to the government interrogators. But it was even more difficult to explain why he would have confessed to his own mother—unless, of course, he actually committed the crime. In other words, the state sold this piece of evidence to the jury "as an unprompted," and therefore a reliable, confession.[12] Of course, this was far from the truth. But truth didn't matter. Wiegert's last-ditch effort to save the confession had worked. To use an analogy from a different sport, his haymaker punch had landed.

By the time Dassey's trial rolled around, Kachinsky had been removed from the case. The trial judge had not been impressed with his defense strategy of letting Wiegert and Fassbender have a fifth go at his client—without even sitting in on the interrogation, no less. But even though new counsel was appointed to defend Dassey, the state's lucky streak was not yet over. Instead, it would continue into the trial itself.

24

GETTING LUCKY AT TRIAL

A s discussed in previous chapters, the state caught a lot of pretrial breaks—some of which came courtesy of pretrial counsel Len Kachinsky. But Dassey's appellate lawyers also argued that the state's undeserved good fortune continued at trial, where Dassey's trial lawyers did, or failed to do, several things that damaged his defense even further.

First, they claimed, the trial lawyers failed to sufficiently demonstrate to the jury that Wiegert and Fassbender contaminated Dassey's so-called confession. More specifically, at trial the prosecutors used the intricate details of Dassey's statements as evidence of his guilt. It was therefore very important to know *where* those details came from. If they came from Dassey, then that would be evidence that the confession was truthful, which is exactly what the prosecutors argued. "During closing, the State also argued that Brendan's confession was corroborated because he said that Halbach had been shot in the head . . . [and] Avery had gone under the RAV4's hood."[1]

The problem, of course, was that these details did *not* come from Dassey. As earlier chapters demonstrated, they came from Wiegert and Fassbender. And the trial lawyers' failure to adequately "call the jury's attention to this contamination" is what allowed the state to successfully (but falsely) paint the confession as being corroborated and, therefore, truthful.[2]

Second, Dassey's trial lawyers agreed to allow the prosecutor to stop playing the March 1 interrogation video right before the child recanted his confession. In the part of the video the jury never saw, Dassey told his mother that he had "confessed only because the police 'got in my head.'"[3] The two trial lawyers were split on whether the jury should see that footage. The view that ultimately prevailed was that "the video showed Brendan's mother believing that her son had committed the crime," and would therefore have been harmful to Dassey's false-confession defense.[4]

The appellate lawyers argued, however, that this was not a reasonable strategic decision; rather, the video actually showed Dassey's mother "challenging his interrogators: 'Were you pressuring him?'"[5] And what could be more important to a false-confession defense than for the jury to see the defendant immediately recanting his alleged confession? "If the jury had seen Brendan's recantation and Barb's reaction, it would have understood that Brendan had credibly asserted his innocence immediately after his interrogation ended."[6]

And third, the trial lawyers never really even put on a true false-confession defense. Citing an article that I coauthored with Danielle Chojnacki and Lawrence T. White, the appellate lawyers argued that jurors simply do not understand why a person would falsely confess to a crime he didn't commit. In fact, our study-turned-article revealed that nearly 74 percent of even highly educated, juror-eligible citizens mistakenly believed an innocent person would either never confess or would only do so after "strenuous pressure."[7]

Wiegert and Fassbender used much softer, but equally effective, interrogation tactics on Dassey; they wisely avoided applying the "strenuous pressure" that jurors associate with false confessions. Given this, the trial lawyers should have called a false-confession expert to testify in Dassey's defense. According to Dassey's appellate lawyers, Lawrence White had already reviewed Dassey's confession for Jerry Buting and Dean Strang in their defense of Avery. Further, they said, Dr. White had even agreed to testify at Dassey's trial. He would have explained to the jury how the interrogators' softer tactics—including leading questions, false promises, and minimization—were known to increase the risk of false confessions.[8]

The appellate lawyers argued that, because the jury never had the benefit of hearing "all of this specialized knowledge about coercion, contamination, and the intricate dynamics of the interrogation process," Dassey's defense was irreparably harmed.[9] That is, the prosecutor was able to argue to Dassey's jury: "The richness of the detail provided by the defendant in that confession tells us that it's true. You can't have that rich of a detail unless you were there, unless you experienced it, unless you lived through it."[10]

Similarly, because the trial lawyers did not show the jury that Dassey recanted as soon as the interrogation ended, and because they did not use an expert witness to explain that the interrogators' tactics were known to produce false confessions, the prosecutor was able to make an even more compelling (but false) claim during the jury trial: "People who are innocent don't confess. The defendant confessed because he was guilty. Because he did it. An innocent person is not going to admit to this."[11]

But as big as these breaks were for the government's case, Wisconsin prosecutors sometimes forget how lucky they are to be plying their trade in the Dairy State. Why? Because most of Wisconsin's trial judges allow prosecutors to convict defendants by a mere preponderance of the evidence standard, and, despite what the United States Constitution guarantees, do not require the state to prove the defendant's guilt beyond a reasonable doubt.

This was true in Dassey's case as well. When the trial judge described the burden of proof to the jury, he explained the term "reasonable doubt." But then, just as Wiegert had told Dassey that anything he said could be used *against* him, and then immediately told him that anything he said would be used *for* him, Dassey's trial judge employed a similar tactic. He took a Wiegert-like, 180-degree turn and told the jury: "you are *not* to search for doubt. You are to search for the *truth*."[12]

Prosecutors love this jury instruction for several reasons. First, any fair-minded person would admit that when you tell the jury the state must prove its case beyond a reasonable doubt, but then tell them not to search for doubt but to search for truth instead, this can only lower the burden of proof. Under Wisconsin's jury instruction, if a juror thought that a charge is merely probably true—also known as the much lower preponderance of evidence standard—he or she would feel obligated to convict. Why? Because the judge just instructed the jury not to search for doubt but to search for the truth. And if the defendant is probably guilty, then a search for the truth requires a conviction.

Prosecutors have long denied this burden-lowering effect, citing a lack of empirical proof to support the claim. So Lawrence White and I conducted and published two controlled studies that demonstrated three things. First, mock jurors who received Wisconsin's jury instruction convicted at significantly higher rates than those who received a legally proper burden-of-proof instruction.[13] Second, mock jurors who received Wisconsin's jury instruction convicted at the identical rate as those who received no reasonable doubt instruction whatsoever.[14] And third, mock jurors who were told "not to search for doubt" but "to search for the truth," as Wisconsin jurors are, were nearly twice as likely to mistakenly believe it was legally proper to convict a defendant even if they had a reasonable doubt about his guilt.[15]

The other reason prosecutors love Wisconsin's pattern jury instruction is that it allows them to cloak themselves in the "truth flag," while dismissing the defense lawyer's arguments as mere attempts to create doubt—something for which the jury should not be searching, according to the instruction. As a Washington court observed, Wisconsin's jury-instruction language "impermissibly portray[s] the reasonable doubt standard as a defense tool for hiding the truth[.]"[16] And here is the ironic part: just as Wiegert and Fassbender hid behind their supposed desire for the truth while strong-arming Dassey into telling them what they wanted to hear, so too do prosecutors claim to be seeking the truth as they try to win convictions at any cost.

For example, if Wisconsin's prosecutors were really after the truth, why did they argue to Steven Avery's jury that only one man—Avery—murdered Halbach, and then argue to Dassey's jury that both he *and* Avery raped and murdered Halbach? One or both of these stories must be false. More significantly, if Dassey's prosecutor really wanted the jury to search for the truth, why would he argue that innocent people don't confess? False confessions were well documented and widely known at the time of Dassey's trial. As his appellate lawyers demonstrated shortly after his conviction, "Hundreds of confessions have been proven false, and many more have been shown to be unreliable. Clinical studies have proven, moreover, that juveniles and the mentally limited are particularly vulnerable" to false confessions.[17]

The prosecutors didn't care that they were using alternating versions of "the truth," depending on which defendant was on trial, in order to win both cases. And Dassey's prosecutors had no interest in the behavioral research on false confessions. When the evidence didn't suit the state, the prosecutor didn't just ignore it, he actually told the jury the opposite: "People who are innocent don't confess."

The jury bought into this sophistry, and it convicted Dassey on all counts. Ironically, in doing so, the jurors may have fallen for the same type of wordplay that Wiegert and Fassbender used to trick Dassey into confessing in the first place.

25

MAILING IN THE APPEAL

I had practiced criminal defense for many years without handling an appeal. Rather, all of my work was at the trial-court level, ranging from pre-charging representation all the way through jury trial and, when necessary, sentencing. But then, many years into my practice, I teamed up with two other lawyers in representing a defendant in an appeal—my first and last.

I wasn't surprised that appellate work was tedious; I had already suspected as much. I had, to that point, avoided appeals because I didn't want to lose sleep wondering if I used the correct color paper for the brief's cover, set my margins exactly right, used a court-approved font, had the appendix in perfect form, or submitted just the right number of copies. As a trial lawyer, I was already losing sleep; I didn't need to add these hyper-technical concerns to the list of things that were keeping me up at night.

Rather, what really turned me away from doing any more appeals was this: We had raised several issues, including an incredibly strong constitutional issue. Yet that particular topic was nowhere to be found in the appellate court's decision. When reading it, my first thought was, "Do I have all the pages, or did I somehow lose one?" When I realized I had the entire decision in my hands, I soon figured out that the appellate court had simply ignored our strongest issue en route to denying our appeal.

And when appellate courts decide that they *will* address a particular issue, they operate, in some respects, like the police. That is, just as interrogators have different tactics for getting suspects to confess to their predetermined version of the truth, appellate courts also have several tactics designed to reach their own predetermined outcome: affirming the defendant's conviction.

First, appellate courts will sometimes acknowledge the defendant's argument, but then simply skip the required legal analysis and just rule against him. For example, when Dassey's appellate lawyers challenged his confession, the role of the appellate court was to conduct a "careful examination of all the circumstances of the interrogation."[1] And the precise issue for the appellate court to decide was whether Dassey's confession was (1) voluntary or (2) coerced by the interrogators' threats, false promises of leniency, and the other tactics. Further, because Dassey was a juvenile, even *more* was required of the court: "His age alone triggers this Court's duty to review his confession with special care."[2]

Dassey's appellate lawyers presented nearly thirty paragraphs in sixteen pages explaining why Dassey's confession was coerced.[3] And this does not include their sections that recapped the confession itself or discussed the related argument that Dassey's trial lawyers were ineffective for the way they handled the confession. So when the appellate court rejected Dassey's argument, how much space did it spend in "careful[ly] examin[ing] all of the circumstances of the interrogation"?

In pages: less than one. In paragraphs: three. Its first of the three paragraphs was canned language that merely recited a couple of case names and stated the applicable rule of law: the court must balance the defendant's "personal characteristics against the police pressures used to induce the statements."[4] This left two paragraphs for actual analysis. Because it is so brief, and because prosecutors are so quick to complain that defense lawyers take things "out of context," it is worth reading the entirety of the court's two-paragraph discussion.

> The trial court heard the testimony of Dassey's mother, his school psychologist and a police interviewer, and had the benefit of listening to the audiotapes and viewing the videotaped interviews. The trial court found that Dassey had a "low average to borderline" IQ but was in mostly regular-track high school classes; was interviewed while seated on an *upholstered couch*, never was physically restrained and was *offered food, beverages* and restroom breaks; was properly Mirandized; and did not appear to be agitated or intimidated at any point in the questioning. The court also found that the investigators used normal speaking tones, with *no* hectoring, *threats or promises of leniency*; prodded him to be honest as a reminder of his moral duty to tell the truth; and told him they were "in [his] corner" and would "go to bat" for him to try to achieve a rapport with Dassey and to convince him that being truthful would be in his best interest. The court concluded that Dassey's confession was voluntary and admissible.

The court's findings are not clearly erroneous. Based on those findings, we also conclude that Dassey has not shown coercion. As long as
investigators' statements merely encourage honesty and do not promise
leniency, telling a defendant that cooperating would be to his or her
benefit is not coercive conduct. Nor is professing to know facts they
actually did not have. The truth of the confession remained for the jury
to determine.[5]

As Dassey's appellate lawyers later argued in federal court, "This
blinkered analysis, devoid of context or completeness, falls short of what
the Supreme Court demands" when assessing whether a confession is
voluntary.[6] But to call this even a "blinkered analysis" is a bit generous.
It really is not an analysis at all. Rather, the state appellate court simply
rubberstamped the trial judge's earlier decision, without even mentioning,
let alone considering, any of the coercive interrogation tactics described in
the earlier chapters of this book.

And any criminal defense lawyer could see the court pulling out its
rubberstamp long before its ink touched the page. How? In the first of
its three paragraphs, the court cautioned that it was loath to "upset a trial
court's determination that a confession was voluntary."[7] It was easy to see
what was coming next: the appellate court never even bothered conducting the analysis that was needed to make a real decision. Rather, its decision was already made.

Second, another of the appellate court's conviction-affirming tactics
is this: as chapter 18 warned, courts love to overemphasize the importance of "food" and "beverages" when deciding whether confessions are
voluntary. Wiegert and Fassbender knew this, which is why they offered
Dassey "a soda" and "a sandwich" so many times they were unable to put
on the brakes: they even offered Dassey's mother "a sandwich" as she
was watching her sixteen-year-old child being hauled off in handcuffs.
The appellate court found the interrogators' generosity, along with the
"upholstered couch," to be of great importance. In fact, these three things
in combination—sandwich, soda, and couch—were probably enough to
seal Dassey's fate.

To appreciate the absurdity of this judicial reasoning—here the word
"reasoning," like the word "analysis," is probably too generous—just
imagine the reverse scenario. Imagine that a defendant was interrogated,

confessed, and was convicted at trial. What if, on appeal, he argued that because he was seated in an uncomfortable folding chair, was not offered any food, and was only given a cup of tap water instead of soda, his statement should have been suppressed? The appellate court would reject that argument faster than Wiegert can read a Miranda warning.

Third, the state appellate court also employed an even more blatant, conviction-affirming trick: whenever it would benefit the state, the court unapologetically concluded that night is day, and vice versa. For example, in the most outrageous part of its two-paragraph disposition, the court simply concluded that the interrogators did not make promises of leniency to Dassey. But in reality, Wiegert and Fassbender repeatedly told him that, by talking, he was helping himself. As chapter 12 illustrated, their promises went on for hours and days, and ran the gamut from the general to the highly specific.

Dassey's appellate lawyers argued that when the appellate court found that Wiegert and Fassbender did not make any promises, it "unreasonably ignored the plain meaning of the interrogators' words. Any kid in Brendan's shoes would have heard, loud and clear, that he would not be in trouble so long as he admitted guilt."[8] Further, Dassey literally thought his interrogators would live up to their end of the bargain. "Brendan's belief that he was going back to school, even after confessing to murder, confirms that [the promise] was sent, received, and relied upon."[9]

And if night is day, then day is night. The appellate court also determined that the interrogators did not threaten Dassey. But as chapter 11 explained, when Wiegert and Fassbender first interrogated him at Mishicot High School without Miranda warnings, they made the following threat to get him talking:

> We've got people back at the sheriff's department, district attorney's office. . . . They're taking about trying to link Brendan Dassey with this event. . . . [T]hey're saying that Brendan had something to do with it or the cover up of it which would mean that *Brendan Dassey could potentially be facing charges for that.* . . . We said no, let us talk to him, give him the opportunity to come forward with the information he has. . . . Talk about it, we're not just going to let you high and dry . . . I promise I will not let you high and dry, I'll stand behind you.[10]

It is difficult to imagine a clearer threat than that. But in appellate-court land, just as the words "I promise I will not let you high and dry, I'll stand behind you," do not constitute a promise, the threat that Dassey "could potentially be facing charges for that" is not a threat. Night is day, and day is night.

These three appellate court tactics cast serious doubt on whether law can even be called a profession. Imagine if a medical doctor or nurse simply decided to change the meaning of words and throw away the anatomy and pharmacology textbooks when treating a patient they viewed as unworthy of their care. That simply does not happen. As many of my colleagues and I have sometimes lamented, "What is the point of having laws, or even language? None of it really matters." That's why, when things are being litigated in the Wisconsin state appellate court system, the prosecutor can, as the saying goes, "mail it in."

One of Dassey's lawyers knew ahead of time that his state court appeal would go nowhere. Steven Drizin used his own baseball analogy: "It would be very difficult for Brendan to get relief in the Wisconsin state court system. This case was just too much of a heater."[11] In other words, Dassey had just confessed to a rape and murder and had been convicted. No matter how coercive the interrogation tactics, and no matter how vulnerable the child defendant, there wasn't an elected judge in the state—and they're *all* elected in Wisconsin—who had the courage to reverse the conviction.

Fortunately for Dassey—as well as for the defendant in my appeal discussed at the beginning of this chapter—state appellate court cases can sometimes work their way into the federal court system. Enter the Honorable William E. Duffin.

Part V
MAKING A FEDERAL CASE OF IT

26

REVERSAL OF FORTUNE

A pretrial motion is, in many ways, like an appeal: both are written requests, based on the facts and the law, for the court to do something. The main difference is that while an appeal is directed to an appellate court, a pretrial motion is directed to a trial judge. As a trial lawyer, I have filed numerous—probably several hundred—pretrial motions. These have included motions to dismiss cases, to exclude irrelevant evidence, and to suppress illegally obtained evidence including coerced confessions.

Prosecutors don't like defense motions. As one prosecutor angrily told me in a candid moment before a court hearing, "Your motions are like boils on my ass!" But while a defense motion may force a prosecutor to read and, once in a great while, file a written response, that's usually the extent of the damage. Trial judges don't often grant defendants' pretrial motions—particularly those that seek to suppress evidence. In some cases, trial judges will deny such motions without any thought at all; their lack of analysis can make the two-paragraph discussion in Dassey's appellate court decision look like a full-length novel by comparison.

However, depending on the trial judge and the nature of the motion, defense lawyers do sometimes win. And the reaction to these victories can include relief, joy, and other positive emotions. But most of all, winning restores a feeling of professionalism to the practice of law. The judge didn't just do whatever he or she wanted. Instead, the judge actually read the motion, thought about the facts, understood the legal principles, and then applied the law—even when doing so hurt the government's case.

These positive emotions must have been what Dassey's lawyers experienced when his appeal moved from the conviction affirming, rubberstamping state appellate court system to the federal court system. The District Court for the Eastern District of Wisconsin did what the state appellate court should have done nearly four years earlier and what

Dassey's trial judge should have done about one decade earlier: suppress Dassey's confession.

To begin his analysis, United States Magistrate Judge William E. Duffin answered the obvious question: Was Dassey's confession *true*?

> [T]he court acknowledges *significant doubts* as to the reliability of Dassey's confession. Crucial details evolved through repeated leading and suggestive questioning and generally stopped changing only after the investigators, in some manner, indicated to Dassey that he finally gave the answer they were looking for. Purportedly corroborative details could have been the product of contamination from other sources, including the investigators' own statements and questioning, or simply logical guesses, rather than actual knowledge of the crime.[1]

But, oddly, while the truth of a confession can be the basis for allowing the state to use it at the defendant's trial, the falsity of a confession cannot be the basis for suppressing it, or keeping it out of trial. Instead, "if a person voluntarily but falsely confesses, it is the jury, not the court, that serves as the check against an innocent person being convicted of a crime he did not commit."[2]

Obviously, Dassey's jury did not protect him from conviction. Ken Kratz and his fellow government agents had executed a well-organized, highly effective media campaign before trial. In so doing, they won over the general public long before the jury set foot in the courtroom. Additionally, Dassey never had the benefit of a false confession expert at trial. This allowed the prosecutor to convincingly (but falsely) argue that "people who are innocent don't confess." So even if Dassey's fate wasn't sealed before his trial began, it certainly was sealed by the time the jury started its deliberations.

Given that the truth of the confession was an issue for the jury, the federal judge had to decide whether Dassey's confession was voluntary. "If a confession is the product of deceptive interrogation tactics that have overcome the defendant's free will, the confession is *involuntary*."[3] And if it is involuntary, then Dassey is entitled to a new trial where the state would not be allowed to use the confession. When determining whether the confession was voluntary or involuntary, the judge must look to "the totality of all the surrounding circumstances—both the characteristics of the accused and the details of the interrogation."[4]

Instead of cherry-picking one or two facts to reach a predetermined outcome, the federal judge actually evaluated "all the surrounding circumstances." He acknowledged that the interrogators seated Dassey on a piece of "upholstered furniture" and offered him "food and beverages."[5] And he acknowledged that some of the other facts recited by the state appellate court, while not important, were also true. For example, the judge agreed that Wiegert and Fassbender "maintained calm tones" when interrogating Dassey.[6] However, "when assessed against all of the circumstances of Dassey's interrogation, these facts are overshadowed by far more consequential facts."[7]

What are these "far more consequential facts"? With regard to Dassey's personal characteristics, they included Dassey's young age, his limited intellectual abilities (even for his age), and his complete lack of experience with the police. The judge also considered that Dassey did not have an adult with him during the interrogations; after all, "it is easier to overbear the will of a juvenile than of a parent or attorney."[8]

And with regard to the interrogators' tactics, the judge recognized that Wiegert and Fassbender exploited Dassey. For example, the judge noticed that the interrogators repeatedly told him they were looking out for him, and even regularly touched him and talked about their role as friends and fathers, not as cops.[9]

However, the real kicker for the judge was the interrogators' repeated false promises. Sure, they employed the simple trick described in chapter 12: they first told Dassey they "can't make any promises" right before unleashing their torrent of promises. But this judge wasn't looking for a form-over-substance trick so he could rubberstamp the conviction. Rather, he looked at the substance of the dozens of promises Wiegert and Fassbender made to Dassey; consequently, the judge was not swayed by their no-promise disclaimer. He realized that this "single, isolated statement was drowned out by the host of assurances that they already knew what happened and that Dassey had nothing to worry about."[10] In this judge's court, it is substance over form that matters. And a promise that wears another label is still a promise.

The judge's analysis of the case law was equally thorough. And, even more frustrating for the prosecutors, he wasn't buying the government's canned, simplistic arguments that the state appellate court hungrily devoured. For example, Dassey's prosecutors had employed this tired trope: to begin, they cited cases where defendants had been interrogated longer than Dassey had been; next, they pointed out that, in those cases, the courts did not suppress the confessions; therefore, they concluded, this judge should not suppress Dassey's confession.

For a defense lawyer, battling this type of argument is like debating a kindergartner on foreign policy in the Middle East. It is incredibly difficult, and probably impossible, to bring your opponent up to the level necessary to even begin a meaningful discussion. As Dassey's appellate lawyers put it: "To argue that false promises made to Brendan must be acceptable because other defendants were detained longer is to compare apples to oranges."[11]

And in the end, the judge agreed: Wiegert and Fassbender "repeatedly claimed to already know what happened . . . and assured Dassey that he had nothing to worry about. These repeated false promises, when considered in conjunction with all relevant factors, most especially Dassey's age, intellectual deficits, and absence of a supportive adult, rendered Dassey's confession *involuntary*."[12]

In other words, Dassey won. His conviction was vacated (or, more accurately, his petition for a writ of habeas corpus was granted) and the state was given ninety days to do one of the following things: (1) "release Dassey from custody"; (2) retry him but without using the so-called confession; or (3) appeal the district court's decision to the Seventh Circuit Federal Court of Appeals.[13]

Regarding option number one—and as I have tried to explain to several fans of *Making a Murderer* who thought Dassey was actually going to walk free—releasing him from custody was off the table from the get-go. The prosecutors were too emotionally invested in this case. They had convinced themselves that Dassey was really guilty and, further, that the police did not violate any of his constitutional rights. There wasn't a federal court judge on Earth that was going to change their minds about any of that. And even *if* the prosecutors believed that Dassey's rights were violated, they still needed to protect their victory or, at the very least, defend the honor of the trial judge and the state appellate court that hand-delivered their victory to them (and would continue to hand deliver more victories to them in the future).[14]

Regarding option number two—retrying the case without the confession—there was no eyewitness or physical evidence linking Dassey to the crime. Ken Kratz pointed out that, in addition to Dassey's now-suppressed statement, he also made earlier statements that could be used at a second trial. The problem with Kratz's argument, however, is that Dassey did not incriminate himself in any of those earlier statements. (If he had, the prosecutor would have piled them up and used them at his first trial.) Therefore, even though the prosecutors firmly believed in Dassey's guilt, they did not want to retry a case without an eyewitness, physical evidence, or a confession. Option number two, therefore, was about as likely as option number one.

That leaves only one choice: option number three. The state would appeal to the Seventh Circuit Court of Appeals. As the next chapter explains, the Seventh Circuit's decision would hinge on a rather strange bit of law called the Antiterrorism and Effective Death Penalty Act.

THE AEDPA
"A FORMIDABLE BARRIER"

If the issue in Dassey's case were whether his confession is true, then Dassey would win hands-down. Not only did the federal judge have "significant doubts as to the reliability" of the confession,[1] but few people, outside of a handful of current and former government agents in Wisconsin, think the confession is true. And even those people are forced to concede that the confession itself is false; they merely contend that Dassey was *somehow* involved in Halbach's death, thus making the conclusion (but not the details) of his confession sort of true.

But unfortunately for Dassey, truth isn't the issue.[2] Instead, the issue is whether his confession was voluntary. If it was not voluntary—in other words, if it was involuntary or coerced—then it should not have been used against him and he is entitled to a new trial. However, as far as the Seventh Circuit Court of Appeals is concerned, that really isn't the issue either. If the Seventh Circuit only had to decide whether the confession was voluntary, Dassey would, once again, win hands-down. But the issue is a bit more muddled—or, to put it more kindly, unnecessarily nuanced.

Dassey's appeal is subject to the standard set forth in the Antiterrorism and Effective Death Penalty Act (AEDPA). For Dassey's case, this applicable law is poorly named; nothing about his case involves terrorism and Wisconsin doesn't use the death penalty. Regardless, with the passage of AEDPA in 1996, "Congress dramatically changed the federal courts' role in reviewing the judgments of state criminal courts."[3] AEDPA now "erects a formidable barrier" for any defendant seeking justice in the federal court after getting unfairly stapled to the wall by a conviction-loving state court system.[4]

More specifically, "a federal court cannot grant a petitioner habeas relief merely because the federal court disagrees, *or even strongly disagrees*, with the state court's decision."[5] Instead, for the Seventh Circuit to side with Dassey, it must agree with Judge Duffin that the Wisconsin Court of

Appeals' opinion was "not merely wrong but *so wrong* that no reasonable judge could have reached that decision."[6]

Despite this high standard, which renders defense victories "rare, even extraordinary,"[7] Dassey appears to be on at least somewhat solid ground. Yet, even putting aside the magnitude of what is at stake here, who would want a matter of *any* significance to hinge on such a bizarre, arbitrary standard? Where is the line between the state court being "merely wrong" versus "so wrong"? Is this even a real distinction? Or is it just more wordplay that can be arbitrarily used to deny a defendant justice? Shouldn't the federal court just get the case right on its merits? Shouldn't it just decide whether the state court was "wrong," period? With regard to the AEDPA, I previously wrote:

> This bizarre scenario seems more like the product of a *Twilight Zone* episode than of a modern system of criminal justice. The linguistics of the whole thing—whether the [state] appellate court was "merely wrong" or "so wrong"—reminds me of the comic strip where the trial judge, a cat, asks the defendant, a dog, whether he pleads "guilty," "really guilty," or "really, really guilty." The difference between Dassey's case and the comic strip, of course, is that the seemingly meaningless distinction in Dassey's case actually makes all the difference in the world.[8]

But ironically, the Wisconsin Court of Appeals' lust to affirm the conviction, combined with its lack of reasoning ability, may be what saves the day for Dassey in federal court. Remember chapter 25 and the criticism of the state appellate court's two-paragraph "analysis"? In that chapter I argued that it really wasn't an analysis at all. The state court, without even looking at any of Wiegert and Fassbender's actual statements to determine whether they constituted substantive promises, merely jumped to its predetermined, analysis-free conclusion: there were no promises of leniency.

That was potentially a big mistake. The state appellate court should have known that skipping the analysis and going straight to the conclusion wouldn't have earned it a passing grade on a law school exam. And its laziness failed the federal court's test, too. Although the AEDPA is designed to give tremendous deference to the state appellate court's analysis, there first has to be some kind of *actual analysis* to which the federal court can defer. If there is none, then the federal court decides the issue from scratch and the heightened AEDPA—sort of, as a practical matter—falls by the wayside.

To summarize, and perhaps to more clearly restate this complex maze of legal gibberish, Judge Duffin first held that Dassey passed the stringent AEDPA test; however, that test is *so* stringent that the Seventh Circuit could, conceivably, reach a different decision. But Duffin also held that, due to the state appellate court's complete lack of analysis, Dassey's claim should really be analyzed under the lower, "pre-AEDPA standard—that is, de novo—because there is no state court analysis to apply AEDPA standards to."[9] And without anything to which the federal court can defer, it may—and in fact must—do its analysis from scratch. In a way, this part of the decision seems to discard the irrational "merely wrong" versus "so wrong" test, and instead apply a more reasonable test that asks a simpler question: Was the state appellate court "wrong"?

The stage has now been set. Will the Seventh Circuit rule for Dassey? Or will it rule for the state? As the next two chapters explain, the answer is yes.

28

TOO CLOSE FOR COMFORT

fter what seemed like forever for the court that is known as "the rocket docket," the Seventh Circuit Court of Appeals finally issued its decision on June 22, 2017. In a too-close-for-comfort 2–1 opinion of a three-judge panel, the Seventh Circuit affirmed the District Court's decision: Dassey's so-called confession was coerced, it should not have been used against him at trial, and Judge Duffin's reversal of the conviction (or, more technically, his granting of the writ) stands.

The Seventh Circuit's decision is 128 pages. Part of the reason it is so long is that there was no state appellate court reasoning to which the court could defer, so it had to analyze everything from scratch. The Seventh Circuit explains:

> The state court of appeals in this case affirmed the trial court's determination that Dassey's confession was [voluntary and admissible]. As the last state court to speak to the issue, it is that court's decision that we review. . . . [A]fter noting the requirement to consider the voluntariness of the confession using the totality of the circumstances test, the state appellate court addressed the voluntariness of the confession in *two short paragraphs*. . . .
>
> A court has not applied the totality of the circumstances test simply by stating its name. . . . *Applying a rule of law does not require much, but it requires more than just parroting the words of the rule.*
>
> In addition to failing to consider the factors in light of the totality of the circumstances, the state appellate court failed to consider some key factors at all, even individually. . . . It is true that "[t]he more general the rule, the more leeway courts have in reaching outcomes in case-by-case determinations." *But the generality of the rule does not mean that a state court may forsake it completely.*[1]

Given that the Seventh Circuit was starting at square one, what factors swayed it to rule in Dassey's favor? The same factors that swayed the

District Court and every person in the world who is not a police detective or prosecutor in the state of Wisconsin. Most significantly, Dassey's statement was not really *his* statement. It was the interrogators' statement. Sure, Wiegert and Fassbender claimed to want honesty. But that was just a word they used to allow the trial judge and state appellate court to conclude that Dassey's confession was admissible.

The Seventh Circuit looked beyond the interrogators' superficial trickery: "Dassey quickly learned that 'honesty' meant telling the investigators what it was that they wanted to hear. When they did not like his answer, they told him things like 'Come on Brendan. Be honest.'"[2] And when Dassey wouldn't immediately change his answer, the interrogators made sure Dassey knew that they, not objective reality, would determine whether he was telling the truth. "I gotta believe in you and if I don't believe in you, I can't go to bat for you."[3]

It was important to Dassey that Wiegert and Fassbender "go to bat" for him, and the interrogators knew this. As chapter 11 explained, they convinced Dassey that the prosecutors and sheriffs wanted to charge *him* for Halbach's death. However, Wiegert and Fassbender—his two new father-figure friends—were on *his* side and could protect him, as long as he told them what they wanted to hear. The interrogators then used their leverage to shape the confession itself. The Seventh Circuit explains:

> As Dassey got closer and closer to the answers the investigators were looking for, his statements were rewarded with affirmations like "that makes sense. Now we believe you," and in doing so, they cemented that version of the facts. But when Dassey deviated from the expected narrative, the investigators either offered no reward, ignored the comments, steered him away, or let him know that they thought he was not telling the truth. In short, as the examples clearly demonstrate, "be honest," "tell the truth," and similar pleas became code for "guess again, that is not what we wanted you to tell us." And "now we believe you" and "that makes sense" became code for "that's what we want to hear. Stop right there."[4]

The part of the Seventh Circuit's decision that was most enjoyable for me, however, was its debunking of the prosecutorial sophistry that we defense lawyers hear on a frequent basis. It was highly entertaining—for me, anyway—to have an appellate court recognize such nonsense and then use logic and reason to destroy it. For example, the Seventh Circuit debunked the state's outrageous claim that Wiegert and Fassbender did not make any promises to Dassey during the interrogation.

> The government makes much of the fact that Wiegert stated at the beginning of the interview, "[w]e can't make any promises," but that one early admonition was countered by hours and hours of subtle and not so subtle declarations otherwise—the death by a thousand cuts. Moreover, Wiegert's full statement was: "We can't make any promises, *but we'll stand by you no matter what you did.*" What would a reasonable person make of an admonition not to count on any promises, *followed immediately by a clear, unconditional promise*? More importantly, what would Brendan Dassey, with his limited intelligence and social skills, think of this admonition linked with a promise?[5]

The Seventh Circuit also blasted the state for its absurd claim that, except for the one leading question featured in *Making a Murderer*, the rest of the interrogation was merely a question-and-answer session without any leading or prompting.

> Although the government concedes that "Who shot her in the head?" was a leading question, it characterizes the rest of the interrogation as a litany of open-ended questions. . . . The many examples we have just cited belie that claim. . . . But these are merely a few of many instances in which investigators explicitly told Dassey what facts he was to report. . . . The investigators even told Dassey what kinds of language he should use.[6]

The state also had the nerve to argue that the physical evidence corroborated Dassey's confession, thus proving its reliability and voluntariness. (This is the kind of night-is-day, day-is-night argument we defense lawyers frequently hear.) The Seventh Circuit saw through this sophistry as well.

> The State also argues that physical evidence corroborated many of the details to which Dassey confessed, but, in fact, *the lack of physical evidence was the weakest part of the State's case.* There was no DNA or other physical evidence linking Dassey to this crime in any way—not a strand of his DNA in the garage, Avery's bedroom, on the RAV4 or its key, on any knives, guns, handcuffs or any other relevant place. Despite descriptions

of a gruesome killing with stabbing, throat cutting, hair cutting, rape, and a shooting, investigators never found a single drop of Halbach's blood, hair or DNA in Avery's not-so-tidy trailer and garage—not on the sheets, mattress, carpet, walls, clothing, garage floor, mechanic's creeper, gun, handcuffs, or bed posts.[7]

The state even tried to wrap itself in the now-familiar "truth flag," claiming that the contradictions within Dassey's story were not created by Wiegert and Fassbender, but by Brendan himself. The state argued, "As with many difficult admissions, the truth did not come out all at once, but little-by-little in fits of honesty."[8] The Seventh Circuit also rejected this argument, once again relying on critical thinking—something that was absent from Dassey's state court decisions.

> [A] careful review of the confession does not reveal this to be a story gaining clarity over time. Unlike the ordinary course of a confession in which the narrative increases in clarity as the suspect reveals more information, this interrogation was just the opposite. Every time the interrogators protested the veracity of Dassey's account or fed Dassey information, his story changed. If one sits in front of the taped confession with a legal pad and tries to sketch out the details and timeline of the crime, the resulting map is a jumble of scratch outs and arrows that grows more convoluted the more Dassey speaks. In fact, despite what the State describes as a detailed confession, it has never been able to map out a coherent timeline of the crime, or to figure out in what order or where many of the events occurred.[9]

In summary, the court held that "Dassey has successfully demonstrated that the state court decision resulted in a decision that was contrary to, or involved an unreasonable application of, clearly established Federal law, as determined by the Supreme Court of the United States."[10]

Dassey wins again! So it's "case closed" or, as Wiegert and Fassbender might say, "ballgame over," right? Not yet. To say that the wheels of justice turn slowly is a colossal understatement. The glacial pace of the judicial system, combined with the state's nearly unlimited resources flowing from taxpayer dollars, means that Dassey's case is far from over.

To begin, the state requested an en banc review by the full Seventh Circuit Court of Appeals, rather than just a three-judge panel. Such full-court reviews are rarely granted. However, against all odds, the Seventh Circuit agreed to the state's request! As a result, Dassey remains in prison while he awaits the full court's decision—a decision that, as chapter 27 explained, will once again hinge on the application of the bizarre, hyper-technical standard known as the Antiterrorism and Effective Death Penalty Act. And even if Dassey wins for a third time in the federal courts—a victory that is far from guaranteed given his razor-thin victory with the three-judge panel—the state could then petition the Supreme Court of the United States for yet another day in court.

Even if the state loses at every turn, it can still retry Dassey—but it must do so without the benefit of his so-called confession. And because there was no other evidence against Dassey, that should spell doom for the state. However, the Seventh Circuit has—so far—left the door open just a tiny crack. Remember when Wiegert and Fassbender interrogated Dassey, at Len Kachinsky's invitation, after Dassey had been arrested and charged? And remember how the interrogators insisted that Dassey call his mother from jail and confess to her "on the phone" so his confession would appear to be distanced from, and untainted by, the government's coercive interrogation tactics?

For some reason, the admissibility of that phone conversation was not raised, or at least not decided, in the course of the appeals process. Therefore, in its three-judge decision, the Seventh Circuit stated that "should the government decide to retry Dassey, the issue of the admissibility of the May 13 telephone call between Dassey and his mother will require a fresh look to determine whether it is the fruit, so to speak, of an involuntarily obtained confessional tree."[11]

It is beyond doubt that Dassey's phone call with his mother is the biggest piece of "fruit" ever to grow on any "confessional tree." But remember this: If Dassey wins the en banc review in the Seventh Circuit, this issue will be litigated in the Wisconsin state courts, not in the federal courts. So we will, no doubt, be treated to entirely new heights of prosecutorial sophistry. It remains to be seen, however, whether the state court will be able to muster more than "two short paragraphs" of legal analysis en route to its decision, should it be required to weigh in on that fruit-of-the-poisonous-tree issue.

But all of that is premature speculation. It may all be irrelevant, depending on what the Seventh Circuit Court of Appeals does next.

29

LAW IS DEAD

On the bitterly cold morning of December 5, 2017, I parked my car, bundled myself up, and battled the strong Wisconsin head-winds as I trudged toward the Center for the Sciences building at Beloit College. I was there to speak to psychology professor Lawrence T. White's students about psychology-based reforms in the criminal justice system. More to the point, I would explain to them the variety of ways that police, prosecutors, and judges thwart those well-intentioned reforms in order to ensure that defendants are convicted of the crimes with which they are charged.

One of my topics was Wisconsin's recording requirement for inter-rogations in criminal investigations. As I explained the different tactics the police sometimes use to circumvent that requirement, someone in the class asked for my prediction in the Dassey case. My response: Dassey would lose the Seventh Circuit's en banc hearing, and, more specifically, he would lose because of the bizarre standard of review set forth in the Antiterrorism and Effective Death Penalty Act (AEDPA).

Due to the bizarre complexity of the issue, a brief recap is in order: The question for the Seventh Circuit is not whether Dassey's confession was true or false—if that were the point of contention, Dassey would win going away. But, strangely, neither will the court be deciding whether Dassey's confession was voluntary or involuntary. Instead, for Dassey to win, the Seventh Circuit must find that the Wisconsin Court of Appeals' decision (that Dassey's confession was voluntary) was "not *merely* wrong but *so* wrong that no reasonable judge could have reached that decision."[1] This malleable distinction between what is "merely wrong" versus what is "so wrong" was specifically designed to render defense victories "rare, even extraordinary," at this stage of the process.[2]

Further recall that there is a related issue lurking beneath the surface. It is true that the AEDPA requires the federal court to give tremendous deference to the analysis of the state appellate court; however, in order to do so, the state appellate court must have done some *actual analysis* to which the federal court can defer. And in Dassey's case, the Wisconsin Court of Appeals never analyzed anything when concluding that his confession was voluntary; rather, it dispensed with the issue in two superficial paragraphs.

To narrow in even further on the precise legal issue, the Seventh Circuit must answer this question: Does the state appellate court's perfunctory recitation of some legal buzzwords constitute a sufficient "analysis" to which the federal court must defer? The three-judge panel of the Seventh Circuit said that it does not. As it previously wrote, "Applying a rule of law does not require much, but it requires more than just parroting the words of the rule."[3] (And, as the court also noted, analyzing juvenile confessions requires special care, so applying the rule of law to Dassey's case requires even greater effort and attention to detail.)

When I made my prediction about the outcome of Dassey's case, little did I know that my words would be put to the test a mere three days later. And, unfortunately, my prediction was correct. On December 8, 2017, in a 4–3 decision—for whatever reason, only seven of the nine judges participated which falls well short of a full-panel review—the Seventh Circuit Court of Appeals reversed Dassey's hard-fought victory.[4] Why? Because of the AEDPA's requirement that a federal court must give great deference to the state court's decision—even when the state court's decision is wrong.

The majority repeated a slight variation of the now-familiar refrain: The AEDPA "was meant to be difficult to satisfy. The issue is not whether federal judges agree with the state court decision or even whether the state court decision was correct. The issue is whether the [state court] decision was *unreasonably* wrong under an objective standard."[5]

But what about the requirement that the state court perform some actual legal analysis, rather than merely "parrot the words of the rule" in two short paragraphs? In a jaw-dropping twist, the Seventh Circuit held that when the Wisconsin Court of Appeals jumped to its conclusion that the trial judge was correct in finding the confession voluntary, it had done enough. More to the point, "State [appellate] court decisions receive significant deference *even if they provide no reasons at all*."[6]

The majority's mind-boggling decision accomplishes two things. First, it reduces the AEDPA standard—a standard that was, in the first place, designed to render defense victories "rare, even extraordinary"—to a new low point that had not previously been imagined, let alone seen. As the three dissenting judges stated, the majority's opinion attempts to "justify this travesty of justice as something compelled by the AEDPA."[7] "But AEDPA does not paralyze us in the face of a clear constitutional violation. . . . This court should be granting [Dassey's] petition for a writ of habeas corpus and giving the state an opportunity to retry him, if it so desires."[8]

And second, the majority's decision essentially relieves Wisconsin's appellate court judges of the obligation to perform any actual legal analysis—the very thing for which they are handsomely paid. (With salaries that approached $140,000 in 2017, plus a smorgasbord of valuable benefits, readers can adapt an AEDPA-like framework of their own and decide for themselves whether these judges are "merely" overpaid or, instead, "grossly" overpaid.)[9]

To put it another way, consider this: When a state appellate court wants to affirm a confessing defendant's criminal conviction, which of the following options is now more enticing? Doing some actual legal analysis, which carries the risk of incorrectly reciting the relevant facts or misapplying the applicable law, thus triggering the AEDPA's "merely wrong" versus "so wrong" test? Or simply skipping the legal analysis altogether and instead rubber-stamping the trial court's ruling, thus avoiding the AEDPA entirely and saving a great deal of time and effort in the process? The choice is clear: State appellate courts can now affirm convictions and avoid reversals in federal court simply by rendering decisions that "provide no reasons at all."

As the philosopher Friedrich Nietzsche might have said about such a bizarre state of affairs, law is dead.[10] And as the dissenters on the Seventh Circuit *did* say, "Dassey will spend the rest of his life in prison because of the injustice this court has decided to leave unredressed."[11]

30

STARE DECISIS

The Latin stare decisis means "to stand by things decided."[1] Today, we simply refer to this concept as following legal precedent. What this means is that whenever a court makes a decision, it is bound by its prior decisions and, especially, the prior decisions of higher courts. This "promotes the evenhanded, predictable, and consistent development of legal principles, fosters reliance on judicial decisions, and contributes to the actual and perceived integrity of the judicial process."[2] In theory, then, it is the very rare case where a court should break from precedent.

Given this reliance on precedent—and putting aside, momentarily, the hyper-technicalities discussed in the last chapter—many people understandably wonder how the Seventh Circuit's panel of seven judges could possibly have ruled 4–3 *against* Dassey. After all, there are numerous court decisions where the interrogators' promises and threats were less extreme than Wiegert's and Fassbender's, yet the defendants' confessions were considered coerced and therefore not admissible. Why didn't the seven-judge panel have to follow those holdings? The answer is that the doctrine of stare decisis has little meaning in real-life criminal cases. In the real world, judges can easily evade it by "distinguishing" prior case law based on the most insignificant factual details.

To illustrate this phenomenon, we will step aside, momentarily, from Dassey's case to one of my own. I first discovered the uselessness of the stare decisis doctrine as a young lawyer defending a man charged with simple misdemeanor possession of marijuana. The facts of the case were undisputed. The police saw my client on the street, had a legitimate reason to suspect he possessed a marijuana cigarette, watched him go into his home, followed him inside without permission and without a warrant, and then searched and arrested him.

This seemed like an obvious Fourth Amendment violation to me. And when drafting my motion to suppress the evidence, I was thrilled to find a case directly on point. The case even had its origins in—where else?—Wisconsin, and it was appealed all the way to the Supreme Court of the United States. I couldn't have dreamed of finding a better case for purposes of legal precedent.

In that case, *Welsh v. Wisconsin*,[3] the facts were also undisputed. The police suspected a man of driving drunk, learned that he had abandoned his car, went to his home, walked inside without permission and without a warrant, and searched and arrested him. Given these facts—facts that were identical to my case in every meaningful way—our nation's highest court ruled as follows:

> It is axiomatic that the physical entry of the home is the *chief evil* against which the wording of the Fourth Amendment is directed. . . . It is not surprising, therefore, that the Court has recognized, as a basic principle of Fourth Amendment law, that searches and seizures inside a home without a warrant are presumptively unreasonable. . . .
>
> Prior decisions of this Court . . . have emphasized that exceptions to the warrant requirement are few in number and carefully delineated, and that the police bear a heavy burden when attempting to demonstrate an urgent need that might justify warrantless searches or arrests. . . .
>
> Our hesitation in finding exigent circumstances, especially when warrantless arrests in the home are at issue, is particularly appropriate when the underlying offense for which there is probable cause to arrest is *relatively minor*. . . . When the government's interest is only to arrest for a *minor offense*, that presumption of unreasonableness is difficult to rebut, and the government usually should be allowed to make such arrests only with a warrant issued upon probable cause by a neutral and detached magistrate. . . .
>
> The Supreme Court of Wisconsin let stand a warrantless, night-time entry into the petitioner's home to arrest him for [suspected drunk driving]. Such an arrest, however, is clearly prohibited by the special protection afforded the individual in his home by the Fourth Amendment. The petitioner's arrest was therefore invalid, the judgment of the Supreme Court of Wisconsin is vacated, and the case is remanded.[4]

Despite this clear legal precedent, the prosecutor wanted a conviction and therefore opposed my motion to suppress the marijuana cigarette. He argued, without articulating any explanation or reason, that the police in my client's case were justified in entering the home and that *Welsh* was distinguishable on its facts. The trial-court judge then turned toward my direction, and our exchange went something like this:

Judge: Mr. Cicchini?

Me: Thank you. I've provided a case directly on point. The prosecutor says it's distinguishable, but doesn't explain why he believes that. *Welsh* is a case from our nation's highest court. It holds that the police cannot walk into a person's home without a warrant to search and arrest him for a "minor offense." That's exactly what the police did to my client. The facts here are not disputed. The police violated the Fourth Amendment and the marijuana cigarette should be suppressed.

Judge: Well, Mr. Cicchini, in *Welsh*, the police were pursuing a man for suspected drunk driving. Your client, as you concede, was suspected of marijuana possession—a suspicion that, you must also concede, turned out to be correct.

Me: With regard to the crime under suspicion, that is not in dispute. But that's not the point. Neither is it the point that the suspicion was reasonable at the time, and even turned out to be correct in hindsight. The legal test is whether the suspected offense is a "minor offense." If it is, the police must get a warrant to enter the home. And simple possession of marijuana is a misdemeanor in our state—a lower-end misdemeanor at that. It even carries a lower penalty than . . .

Judge: Well, the Court's language you are referring to seems like dictum to me. It's really not part of the Court's holding.

Me: The Supreme Court of the United States is not going to set down a rule of law that is so limited in its application. The test is whether the suspected offense was minor. If it was, then the entry into the home without a warrant—"the chief evil against which the wording of the Fourth Amendment is directed"—was illegal and the evidence must be suppressed. The Fourth Amendment protects everyone, not just those suspected of drunk driving.

Judge: Well, I see significant differences.

Me: Your honor, this may be helpful. The Court even enumerated many types of suspected crimes that would be too minor to justify a warrantless entry. For example, the Court . . .

Judge: Alright, I'm prepared to rule. The case cited by the defense is applicable only to warrantless entry into the home to arrest a person for suspected drunk driving. In our case, the defendant was suspected of possessing an illegal controlled substance. *Welsh* is distinguishable on those grounds, and the defendant's motion to suppress the evidence is denied.

It really was that easy for a trial-court judge to bypass the doctrine of stare decisis and even the United States Supreme Court—all for the purpose of sinking a defendant who possessed a marijuana cigarette. And even if my client had been suspected not of pot possession but of drunk driving, as was the defendant in *Welsh*, the local judge could have found other insignificant differences on which to hang his hat. For example, in *Welsh*, the police entered the defendant's home at night; in my case, they entered during daylight hours. In *Welsh*, the door was locked and the police ordered the defendant's minor child to open it so they could enter; in my case, the door was shut but unlocked, so they opened it themselves and then walked in. The list of insignificant factual differences goes on and on, all the way down to the defendants' hair color.

Returning, then, to Dassey's case, this type of judicial chicanery was also on full display, but with far more at stake. To begin, when the three-judge panel of the Seventh Circuit ruled in favor of Dassey by holding that his confession was coerced, it analyzed legal precedent extensively. It discussed at least seven cases in depth, and cited more than a half-dozen others, before reaching its decision.[5]

How, then, did the subsequent panel of seven judges respond to this analysis of precedent? Much like the trial-court judge in my marijuana cigarette case, it simply "distinguished" the legal precedent that it did not wish to follow. It then declared that "Dassey simply has not pointed to Supreme Court precedent that mandates relief *under these circumstances*. . . . [T]he Supreme Court has not found a confession involuntary in circumstances like Dassey's March 1st confession."[6] It then elaborated by discussing two cases.

First, the majority of the seven-judge panel believed that *Boulden v. Holman* was instructive. The defendant in that case was older than Dassey and was interrogated for a shorter period of time, two factors what would seem to weigh in Dassey's favor. However, the majority of Dassey's panel found that particular case more troubling than Dassey's, in part because that defendant "was interrogated from 10 p.m. until after midnight after several hours in custody."[7] And because the court in that case held that the defendant's statement was admissible, then Dassey's should be admissible too.

Second, the majority of the seven-judge panel also relied on *Fare v. Michael C.* The defendant in that case was the same age as Dassey, but had a higher IQ and, unlike Dassey, had prior experience with the police. These two factors would seem to weigh heavily in Dassey's favor. However, the majority of Dassey's panel found that particular case more troubling than Dassey's because that defendant "claimed he feared police coercion and pointed out that he wept during the interrogation."[8] And because the court in that case held that the defendant's statement was admissible, then Dassey's should be admissible too.

The three dissenters on Dassey's seven-judge panel were as flabbergasted by this annihilation of precedent as I was when my trial-court judge rubberstamped the warrantless police entry into my client's home to search for his marijuana cigarette. The three dissenters in Dassey's case wrote:

> The majority concedes that AEDPA does not require a "nearly identical factual pattern" to find that a decision involved an unreasonable application of law. But that is in essence what the majority has demanded. In arguing that even non-AEDPA cases have found confessions voluntary under similar circumstances, the majority cites *two decisions*. But as it concedes, *Fare v. Michael C.* is critically different: Michael C. was of average intelligence and had many prior interactions with the criminal justice system. While *Boulden v. Holman* may superficially appear to be more similar to Dassey's case, it is of dubious relevance given the fact that it was decided (along with *Michael C.*) decades before the Supreme Court instructed lower courts to recognize the unique psychological vulnerabilities of youth stemming from their incomplete neurological development.
>
> The Wisconsin Court of Appeals failed . . . to apply in any meaningful way at least three principles that the Supreme Court has clearly established: (1) special care for juvenile confessions, (2) consideration of the totality of the circumstances, and, most importantly, (3) prohibition of psychologically coercive tactics. This led to the kind of extreme malfunction in the adjudication of Dassey's case for which [the law] provides a remedy. By turning a blind eye to these problems, the majority has essentially read habeas corpus relief out of the books.[9]

In short, while the Latin phrase stare decisis sounds impressive, and gives law school professors something to wax eloquent about to the impressionable first-year law students placed in their charge, it offers a criminal defendant little to no help in the real world. The doctrine completely fails to constrain judges at all levels of the court system—from state-level trial courts all the way through federal courts of appeal—and can be sidestepped merely by pointing to the smallest of irrelevant factual differences between cases.

In this way, the law is no different than any other realm of life. A person (here, a judge) first decides the outcome he or she wants to reach, and then cherry-picks the information (here, from previous court decisions) that supports that predetermined conclusion—all other evidence be damned. Or, as the great Ambrose Bierce wrote more than a century ago, under the doctrine of stare decisis, "a previous decision . . . has whatever force and authority a Judge may choose to give it, thereby greatly simplifying his task of doing as he pleases."[10]

31

WHAT IF?

An incredibly long sequence of events had to happen for Brendan Dassey to be convicted of murder without an eyewitness, a single piece of evidence, or even an accusation against him. An even longer sequence of events had to occur for that truly bizarre conviction to eventually be upheld by a flip-flopping federal court of appeals.

It is interesting to imagine how Dassey's life would have turned out if just one of the things in that long chain of causal events had been just the slightest bit different. For example, what if, after Steven Avery's wrongful conviction in the Penny Beerntsen case in the mid-1980s, Dassey's parents had taught him never to speak to law enforcement without an adult present? What if they had taught him simply to say "I want a lawyer" when questioned by any government agent?

Even without such parental wisdom being imparted, what if Dassey had simply thought to tell Wiegert and Fassbender that he wanted his mother present when they questioned him about Teresa Halbach's murder? If Barb had been there, would the interrogators have used the same threats and false promises? Or would they have developed a completely different approach to the interrogation? And would it have worked?

And even without that, what if, when Wiegert and Fassbender first yanked Dassey out of his classroom for a "non-custodial interrogation," Dassey had said, "I don't know anything about how Halbach died and I'm going back to class now"? Or what if Dassey had decided not to speak to the investigators simply because he knew they were trying to gather evidence to pin on his uncle, Steven Avery, for Halbach's murder? In other words, what if Dassey's sense of loyalty to his uncle had overcome his reluctance to tell two adult authority figures to pound sand?

It's also interesting to think about the lawyers. What if the Wisconsin State Public Defender (SPD) had been paid more than $40 per hour—a rate that is *still* in effect in 2018 and is the lowest in the country[1]—to defense lawyers who defend homicide cases? If the pay had been higher, would the SPD have been able to appoint a different, more experienced lawyer than Len Kachinsky to represent Dassey? And how would that have affected the eventual outcome in the case?

Regarding Kachinsky, what if he had talked to Dassey and investigated the case *before* deciding on his defense strategy and sharing it with the media? What if he had been trained in, or at least knew about, the phenomenon of false confessions? And what if, on appeal, Dassey's appellate lawyers had simply alleged that Kachinsky rendered "ineffective assistance of counsel" instead of their claim that he had a "conflict of interest"—a novel theory that was rejected by the District Court and the three- and seven-judge panels of the Seventh Circuit? Given what Kachinsky did and didn't do in the case, would arguing "ineffective assistance of counsel" have been more persuasive to the Seventh Circuit than the claim that Dassey's confession was coerced? Or would the outcome have been the same either way?

Eventually, Kachinsky was removed from the case and the SPD appointed two, more experienced lawyers for Dassey's trial. But those lawyers may have viewed the situation more as defending a "murder case" than a "false confession" case. What if, instead, the trial lawyers had used an expert witness to educate the jury about the interrogation tactics that have a demonstrable link to false confessions? Would that expert have made a difference in the jury's decision? Or was Dassey's ship sunk either way?

What if the Wisconsin Court of Appeals had written only one paragraph, instead of two, when it jumped to its predetermined conclusion that Dassey's confession was freely and voluntarily given? Would that still have been a sufficient analysis to which the federal courts must defer? And what if the Antiterrorism and Effective Death Penalty Act was never signed into law? Would the Seventh Circuit have ruled in Dassey's favor if it didn't have to apply that bizarre "so wrong" versus "merely wrong" standard of review? Or would the seven-judge panel, like the state court of appeals, still have found a way to rule against Dassey?

What if the Seventh Circuit had used a true full-panel review of nine judges instead of seven? That is, what if Judges Flaum and Barrett had also participated in the Seventh Circuit's en banc hearing of Dassey's case? How would they have voted? And what if Judge Richard Posner hadn't retired from the Seventh Circuit shortly before the court issued its decision? How would he have voted and would his vote have made a difference?

And, of course, the biggest remaining question is this: What if the Supreme Court of the United States agrees to hear Dassey's case? Getting the attention of the nation's high court is a long shot, to be sure. But while it *might* be too late for Dassey—check the Postscript section at the end of the book for an update—what types of legal reforms could save other defendants from a similar fate?

Part VI
LEGAL REFORM

32

REFORMING MIRANDA

How do we begin reforming the system to protect innocent suspects from falsely confessing? The logical place to start is with the Miranda warning. Chapter 6 explained why the interrogator is the worst person to read a suspect his Miranda rights: the interrogator's interests are at direct odds with the suspect's. That is, the interrogator's goal is to get the suspect to waive the right to remain silent and the right to a lawyer. However, it is nearly always in the suspect's best interest to invoke one or more of those rights.

Chapters 7 and 8 then demonstrated how this conflict of interest plays out. Because interrogators are motivated to get the suspect talking, they have developed numerous strategies to avoid reading the Miranda warning in the first place and to induce the suspect to waive those rights when they do read it. These tactics include minimizing the importance of the warning, reading the warning quickly to reduce the suspect's comprehension of it, and not giving the suspect the option of actually invoking the rights described in the warning.

Then there are problems with the warning itself. As previous chapters also explained, many versions of the warning are internally inconsistent and nonsensical. And most versions leave out important information that the suspect would need in order to make an informed decision about whether to invoke the rights. But even in the best-case scenario—a slow, clear reading of a "good" version of the warning—Miranda simply contains too much information for an overwhelmed suspect to absorb and process at one time. And bombarding a suspect with all of the information at once further reduces comprehension.

More specifically, "[d]ifferent rights are relevant at different stages of the suspect-police encounter."[1] For example, "the right to stop answering questions once questioning has begun cannot possibly become an issue until the suspect has decided to waive his right to silence in the first place."[2] Similarly, "the right to have an attorney present during questioning is a moot point if the suspect decides to invoke his right to silence."[3]

Given the numerous problems with the existing Miranda warning and the way interrogators present it to suspects, the following section proposes a new Miranda warning. This warning could be adopted at the local level by law enforcement agencies that are concerned about false confessions and wrongful convictions. But because the police do not want suspects to understand and invoke their rights, this is not likely to happen. Fortunately, however, the new warning could (and should) be adopted at the state level, by state legislatures or supreme courts. And, of course, the new warning could also be adopted on a national level. The United States Supreme Court already requires the police to read suspects a Miranda warning; it could easily require them to read a meaningful one.

I first proposed this new Miranda warning in my article—appropriately titled "The New Miranda Warning"—published in the *Southern Methodist University Law Review* in 2012. This chapter reproduces a portion of that article, with minor modifications.[4] The proposed warning is broken out into three forms. Each form contains the language that the interrogator would be required to read to the suspect. Each form then includes additional instructions for the interrogator to follow. Finally, following each form is a discussion section intended for the reader of this book (not the interrogator) that explains how that part of the proposed warning is designed to constrain police abuses, to communicate the suspect's rights more clearly, or to otherwise improve the Miranda process. The proposed Miranda warning begins with Form 1 and, if necessary, proceeds to additional forms after that.

Miranda Warning—Form I

I would like to ask you questions about [describe reason for questioning]. Before I ask you questions, however, I need to inform you of some *very important rights* that you have.

First, you have the right to remain silent. If you decide to talk to me, anything you say can be used *against* you in court. However, if you decide to remain silent, your silence *cannot* be used against you in any way.

If you know that you want to remain silent, I will stop the interrogation now. But if you want to talk to me or if you are not sure whether you

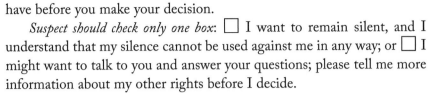

want to talk to me, I will tell you about some additional rights that you have before you make your decision.

Suspect should check only one box: ☐ I want to remain silent, and I understand that my silence cannot be used against me in any way; or ☐ I might want to talk to you and answer your questions; please tell me more information about my other rights before I decide.

Instructions to interrogator: If the suspect checked the first box and elected to remain silent, *end the interrogation now*. If the suspect checked the second box, *proceed to Form 2* to explain additional Miranda rights.

Discussion of Form I

Telling the suspect that the rights are "very important" will alert him that these are not mere bureaucratic formalities, but instead are worthy of his full attention. For this same reason, it is critical to require the police to present the form in writing and to read it verbatim. Any "supplementing" of the form with additional (mis)information could easily defeat Miranda's purpose. Further, taking away the creative liberties of the police by requiring a verbatim reading is not overly burdensome. While refraining from additional, often contradictory, commentary is a bit more challenging for the police, they are capable of such restraint—especially with the threat of suppression of the suspect's statement looming over their heads.

The heart of this form then advises the suspect of his right to remain silent and that anything he says can be used against him—*not for him*—in court. Just as importantly, however, it also advises the suspect that his silence cannot be used against him in any way. This provides full information about the consequences of the suspect's decision and thwarts any implication that talking can somehow be to the suspect's benefit or that not talking can be to his detriment.

This form also tells the suspect what will happen if he chooses to remain silent: The interrogation will end. It then instructs him precisely how to affirmatively invoke the right: Check the box. Importantly, this form provides the suspect with a true choice, unlike many police forms that provide only a directive to sign and waive the rights with no alternative.

Part One of the new Miranda warning focuses on, and stops with, the first of the Miranda rights. This tiered structure puts the spotlight squarely on the only relevant topic at this point in the suspect-police encounter: *the right to remain silent*. If the suspect chooses to invoke this right, then the other rights do not apply. There is no reason to inform him of his right to stop answering questions because he has just elected not to start answering questions. He will be informed of his right to an attorney, and may even be appointed an attorney, when he is brought to court, and there is no need to inform him of his right to have an attorney present at an interrogation in which he just declined to partake. Further, by ignoring these presently irrelevant rights, we avoid using a warning that is long, complex, and obscures the right to remain silent.

Miranda Warning—Form 2

I will now inform you about additional rights that you have.

You have the right to an attorney. If you cannot afford an attorney, the judge will give you one for free if and when you go to court.

You have the right to consult with your attorney before you decide whether you want to talk to me. If you consult with your attorney and decide to talk to me, you have the right to have your attorney with you when you talk to me.

Suspect should check only one box: ☐ Knowing these additional rights, I want to remain silent, and I understand that my silence cannot be used against me in any way; or ☐ I understand these additional rights, but I want to talk to you and answer your questions now, without an attorney.

Instructions to interrogator: If the suspect checked the first box and elected to remain silent, *end the interrogation now*. If the suspect checked the second box, *proceed to Form 3*.

Discussion of Form 2

Because the suspect did not invoke the right to silence after reading the first form, the information in Form 2 becomes relevant. It informs the suspect of all aspects of the right to counsel—the right to counsel itself, the right to court-appointed counsel for the indigent, and the right to consult with counsel before and during any statements to police—and then gives the suspect the *actual option* of remaining silent or talking to the police, rather than a directive to waive the right and speak.

Importantly, this form does not state, or even imply, that this is the suspect's last chance to talk to police or, conversely, that if he chooses to talk to the police an attorney will be made available on the spot. The police have no way of providing counsel prior to or during the interrogation, nor are they obligated to do so. This form is therefore both complete and accurate with regard to the underlying rights and procedure.

Miranda Warning—Form 3

You have told me that you want to give up certain rights and talk to me. I will need you to sign and fill in the information below before we get started. The rights that you are giving up by talking to me are:

The right to remain silent. Again, if you decide to remain silent, that cannot be used against you.

The right to consult with an attorney before and during questioning.

Waiver of Rights: I have decided to talk to you about [describe reason for questioning]. I understand that anything I say can be used against me in court. Finally, I also understand that I can change my mind and stop this interrogation at any time by telling you "I want to stop answering questions." [Suspect to sign, date, and time here.]

Discussion of Form 3

This form recaps the rights the suspect is giving up, reminds him that anything he says can be used against him, and documents the waiver in writing. Most significantly, it informs the suspect of the last of the Miranda warnings: the right to stop talking at any time.[5]

While reforming Miranda is a big step in protecting suspects from coercive police interrogations and false confessions, it is just the beginning. As the next chapter explains, in cases where suspects waive their rights and decide to speak, reforms are desperately needed for the post-Miranda interrogation as well.

33

ROLE-PLAYING INTERROGATORS

While the last chapter offered a highly specific and easily implemented reform measure, this chapter takes a different approach. It builds upon the framework that is currently used to decide whether a confession is admissible at trial. In so doing, it highlights a fundamental flaw in the way that courts analyze this issue.

Earlier chapters explained that when the police interrogate a suspect and obtain a confession, whether that confession is admissible at the suspect-turned-defendant's trial depends on whether the statement was voluntary. A statement is voluntary when the suspect made a rational choice to confess. A statement is not voluntary when, for example, the interrogators dupe the suspect with false information that prevents him from making a rational choice. And the most common way interrogators interfere with a suspect's ability to make a rational decision is to play the role of defense lawyer.

Despite their warning that "anything you say can be used against you," Wiegert and Fassbender seamlessly slipped into the opposite role and played Dassey's advocate. Then, after winning his trust, they provided him with bad advice specifically designed to prevent him from making a rational choice.

For example, the interrogators assured Dassey that talking was in his best interest; in fact, it was required if he wanted their protection from the bad government agents who supposedly were going to prosecute him. The interrogators told him they had a lot of evidence and already knew what happened. They also told him that even if he admitted to helping Avery commit the crimes, he would still be better off if he confessed. They repeatedly told him the crime was not his fault; rather, it was Avery's fault. And they convinced him that, if he just confessed his involvement—involvement they already knew about anyway—he could put this case behind him and even get back to school. After ripping through the

Miranda warning in the squad car on the fateful day of March 1, 2006, Wiegert said:

> All right, ah, so like I told you, we're going to take a ride over to the Manitowoc Sheriff's Department. They've got a nice quiet room there, there's no kids running in and out and stuff, so, and *if you play it right, who knows, maybe we'll get you back as soon as we can.* If we, we all get over there as soon as we can. Um, I'm just gonna have you initial actually also um, here and here, saying that I read you those [rights] and then that you agreed to talk with us, OK? All right.[1]

We know two things for sure. First, the interrogators believed that playing the role of Dassey's advocate would work. Why else would they have spent all of that time building his trust and then lying to him about the consequences of making a statement? And second, we know that playing the role of Dassey's advocate did, in fact, work. He trusted them, believed them, and clearly thought he was going back to school after he gave them the statement they wanted.

Despite all of this, the trial court and the state appellate court found that Dassey's statement was voluntary—the product of a free and rational choice. If, as I have argued before, these courts were merely rubberstamps designed to aid the state in obtaining and preserving its conviction, then nothing I propose in this chapter will change that. On the other hand, if I am wrong, and if these courts actually made a good faith effort to arrive at a reasoned decision, then their absurd conclusion—that the interrogators' lies and promises did not interfere with Dassey's rational decision-making process—proves that the legal framework for this analysis is defective.

Instead of the existing framework, then, we should be using this framework: When the interrogators want to play the role of the suspect's defense lawyer, they should be held to the same standard as the suspect's defense lawyer.

Imagine, for example, that instead of talking to Wiegert and Fass-bender, Dassey had mustered the courage to tell them to get lost and instead hired a lawyer. Then, pretend that the state charged Dassey with rape, murder, and mutilating a corpse, even though it had no physical evidence, eyewitness, or, in this hypothetical scenario, confession. Finally, imagine that Dassey's hypothetical lawyer gave him advice about entering a guilty plea in court that was similar to the advice Wiegert and Fass-bender gave him about admitting guilt in the interrogation room.

That is, just as Wiegert and Fassbender urged Dassey to disregard the Miranda warning they just read to him, suppose the defense lawyer urged Dassey to disregard the warning in the plea form. "Brendan, the form you're signing states that you can be sent to prison if you plead to these crimes. But don't worry, that's not true. That is just meaningless boilerplate. You will help yourself by pleading guilty in court."

Similarly, just as Wiegert and Fassbender told Dassey that he was not legally responsible for assisting Avery, and therefore he could tell them anything and everything without consequence, suppose the defense lawyer gave Dassey similar advice. "Brendan, the law says that because this whole thing was Avery's idea, only he can be held responsible. So even if you plead guilty, thereby admitting to the judge that you helped Avery, you're gonna be okay."

Finally, just as Wiegert and Fassbender lied to Dassey about the evi-dence they had—and what would and wouldn't happen if he simply told them what they already knew—suppose the defense lawyer did the same thing. "Brendan, the state has DNA evidence that proves your guilt, and we already know what happened here. You did help Avery. But again, these crimes are on him, so just admit your role by pleading guilty and you can get back to school."

If Dassey had admitted guilt in court based on this type of advice, his inevitable question to the judge—"Do you think I can get back to school by one twenty-nine?"—would have been met with a smirk and an armed escort to prison. However, if things had actually played out that way, Dassey would also have been allowed to withdraw his guilty plea. Why? Because his hypothetical defense attorney's performance would have been "ineffective." The attorney's advice would not have lived up to the guarantee described in *Strickland v. Washington*.[2] Rather, such advice (1) would not have been accurate; and (2) would have affected Dassey's rational decision-making process with regard to whether he should plead guilty in court.[3]

The questions, then, are these: If Wiegert and Fassbender are allowed to dupe a child by playing the role of his advocate, why shouldn't they be held to the same standard as a defense lawyer? Why shouldn't the duped child be allowed to withdraw his confession, just as a misinformed defendant would be allowed to withdraw his plea? If Wiegert and Fassbender had been held to this standard—a standard quite appropriate for the role they were playing—their misinformation would have rendered Dassey's statements involuntary and therefore inadmissible in court.

This line of thinking, while rational, is admittedly outside the proverbial box. So for a more realistic reform recommendation involving the government's use of a defendant's statements, we must now move from the interrogation room to the courtroom.

FALSE CONFESSION EXPERTS AT TRIAL

Before 2011, whenever a Wisconsin prosecutor wanted to use an expert witness to help convict a defendant at trial, the expert merely had to pass the "mirror test": if the judge put a mirror by the expert's nose and mouth, and the mirror fogged up, the expert could testify. And the prosecutor had a so-called expert on call for just about every situation. For each type of case—for example, child abuse, domestic violence, or drug possession—the prosecutor would file the same useless, canned, typo-ridden "summary of expert testimony," no matter the facts in the particular case being tried.

Did the alleged victim delay reporting the crime until several months or even years later? There's an expert for that. Such delayed reporting is "very common" among victims of the crime for which the defendant is being prosecuted.

Did the alleged victim recant the allegation by saying that he or she made it up while in a drunken state of anger? Don't worry, there's an expert for that, too. Recantations are "very common" among victims who, often, are forced by defendants to recant the truth.

Did the defendant refuse to answer questions when approached by the police? There is definitely an expert for that. Such *pre*-Miranda silence demonstrates a "consciousness of guilt" and is "very common" among people who commit the type of crime for which the defendant is on trial.

But the law states that whether a witness's testimony is true and whether the defendant is guilty are matters to be decided by the jury, not a government agent or a "victim advocate" posing as an expert. So the way prosecutors got away with this scam was to stop just short of having the expert testify, for example, that "the victim's initial accusation, not the recantation, is true," or "the defendant is a liar." Instead, the expert would give his or her spiel to the jury, and then the prosecutor would repeat that testimony in closing arguments to convince the jury, through argument, that the defendant is guilty. It's a hyper-technical distinction, and one that makes no sense anywhere outside of appellate court decisions.

But the bigger problem is that these experts weren't experts at all. Not only were they typically full-time government employees, but they had little, if any, interest in truth. Instead, they were chameleon-like creatures, changing their testimony to fit the facts of any given case to help the prosecutor win a conviction.

For example, suppose the alleged victim *immediately* reported the alleged crime, rather than delaying his or her report. The expert would now testify that immediate reporting was "very common," and the phenomenon of delayed reporting suddenly became merely "possible" or something that "could be" common.

Similarly, suppose the alleged victim did not recant the accusation but instead *changed* the details of the incident, adding to them as time passed. The expert would now brand this mode of piecemeal reporting as "very common." Recantations—though previously a commonality—were now described as anomalous.

And the most chameleon-like experts of all were the police. Suppose that, instead of clamming-up upon seeing the police, the defendant became nervous and talkative. This behavior, according to the officer's testimony, was suddenly the sign of a guilty mind, while silence was a "less common" phenomenon.

Then, in 2011, the law changed in Wisconsin. Instead of the wild frontier, anything-goes approach to expert witnesses, the trial judge was supposed to be a gatekeeper of sorts. By adopting the more stringent federal Daubert standard of admissibility, judges were supposed to shield jurors from faux experts who modified their testimony to suit the prosecutor's needs.[1]

Prosecutors were, quite obviously, not the ones driving this change to the Daubert standard; they liked things exactly as they were. And the criminal defense bar certainly didn't have the clout to bring about this type of change. I didn't know who had advocated for this legal reform—the rules on expert testimony also applied to civil cases, so I suspected Big Business was sailing the ship of change—but many criminal defense lawyers were hopeful that Daubert would change things for the better. Many thought it might put an end to the state's practice of using a government agent or victim advocate to put the gloss of expert testimony on an otherwise weak government case.

I, however, complained aloud that this new law would change nothing for the prosecutor and would only create obstacles for defense lawyers. And I was right. First, with regard to the *prosecutor's* use of these types of experts:

> In theory, Wisconsin's new test for the admissibility of expert testimony "is flexible but has teeth." In practice, it's flexible and has dentures. *Literally every [defense] challenge litigated on appeal since [Daubert] became effective has failed.* The court of appeals has held that expert testimony regarding the retrograde extrapolation of a person's blood alcohol concentration passes Daubert. So does a doctor's testimony based solely on his personal experience with prenatal and delivery case. So does a social worker's testimony based solely on her observations of behavior in child abuse victims. And now . . . so does expert testimony by a drug recognition evaluator.[2]

In other words, the law changed nothing on the prosecutorial side. To use one of the above examples, Wisconsin courts are still allowing government social workers to testify, based solely on their anecdotal experiences, about the commonalities of abused children. Then, based on that testimony, the prosecutor is still arguing that the child in the case being tried is truly a victim and, therefore, the defendant is guilty.

But what about defendants' false confession experts? Given the above examples of how easily the state's experts pass the new Daubert test, it should be a slam-dunk that false confession experts are allowed to testify for the defense, right?

False confession experts are experts in the truest sense of the word. They have PhDs in psychology. They conduct studies that test hypotheses. Their testimony is based on research that is actually published. They have specialized knowledge about the police interrogation tactics and suspects' personal characteristics that are correlated with known false confessions. They have studied false confessions both in real-life criminal cases and in controlled experiments. In short, these witnesses can debunk the state's sophistry in closing argument where the prosecutor cries out to the jury, "People who are innocent don't confess!"

Of course, despite their frequent claim that trials are a search for the truth, prosecutors vigorously oppose defendants' use of false confession experts. Prosecutorial arguments to prevent them from testifying are tired, recycled, invalid, and even nonsensical. Here are three of the most common.

First, before an expert is allowed to testify at trial, he or she must possess specialized knowledge outside the jury's common knowledge. And this makes sense, because if the so-called expert's topic is already within the jury's common knowledge, then there is no need for an expert. Given this, prosecutors shamelessly argue that the phenomenon of false confessions and the factors that are correlated with them already fall within jurors' common knowledge.

This argument can only be described as disingenuous. If false confessions and their causes are within the common knowledge of the typical jury, wouldn't psychologists with PhDs find better things to do with their time? Why would they keep studying something that is known and understood not only within the scientific community but also by non-experts that sit on juries?

And if the body of research on false confessions was already common knowledge, why would prosecutors argue to juries that "people who are innocent don't confess"? If it were commonly known, as prosecutors contend, that innocent people do confess, then prosecutors would not contradict common sense and argue the opposite to the jury. In reality, of course, the commonly held (but erroneous) belief is that an innocent person would never admit to something he didn't do. Prosecutors craft their arguments to take advantage of this misconception. And false confession experts are needed to debunk this fallacy.

Even empirical evidence supports the obvious conclusion that false confession experts have knowledge falling outside of jurors' common knowledge. In a published study-turned-article, Danielle Chojnacki, Lawrence T. White, and I empirically demonstrated that even highly educated survey respondents held serious misconceptions about false confessions and the interrogation tactics that produce them. In other words, there is a large gap between (1) the common knowledge of juror-eligible citizens and (2) the specialized knowledge that PhDs have acquired by reading published studies and conducting their own research.[3] There are no surprises here, so let's move on to the next prosecutorial argument.

Second, prosecutors have literally argued that false confession experts should be prevented from testifying because they might confuse the jury. How? Jurors might believe that the suspect-turned-defendant's confession is false.

The problems with this argument are as obvious as the argument is invalid. It is true that the law does permit the judge to exclude marginally relevant evidence when it is outweighed by the risk of jury confusion.[4] However, the state's argument that a false confession expert would confuse the jury misuses the words "jury confusion"—something that could happen when the jury hears evidence not directly related *to* the charged crime—to describe the possibility that the jury might acquit the defendant *of* the charged crime.

In other words, the state begins by assuming the very thing it has to prove at trial: the defendant is guilty. It then argues that any defense evidence challenging this assumption is "confusing." The prosecutor may as well remove this thin disguise and simply say what he means: any evidence that could raise reasonable doubt about the defendant's guilt should be excluded. The next step, of course, would be to skip the trial entirely and simply ask the defendant whether he pleads "guilty" or "really guilty" to the charged crime.

Third and finally, prosecutors also oppose the use of false confession experts by arguing that, even if the body of research on false confessions is specialized knowledge, the expert is not able to tell the jury whether this particular defendant—the one on trial—falsely confessed.

Well, that's true, but this argument overlooks two things. By comparison, when the prosecutor calls an expert witness to testify, for example, about the factors associated with victim recantations, that expert is not capable of determining whether the particular alleged victim (who testified at trial) lied when making the initial accusation or lied when recanting in court. Despite this, the expert is still allowed to testify.

Additionally, whether a defendant lied when admitting guilt in the interrogation room *or* when denying guilt at trial is an issue for the jury, not the expert, to decide. The law specifically prohibits a false confession expert from testifying about whether, and when, this particular defendant was not telling the truth.[5] Therefore, prosecutors are arguing that false confession experts should not be allowed to testify because they are incapable of doing what the law prevents them from doing anyway. This argument is as absurd as the prosecutors' first two arguments.

But what does all of this have to do with legal reform? In cases where the state uses the defendant's confession as evidence against him, and the defendant claims that he falsely confessed, defense counsel must be permitted to call a qualified expert witness to discuss the body of research on false confessions. The expert's role is to educate the jury, not to opine whether the particular confession at issue is false. Deciding truth or falsity is the jury's role; however, it cannot properly do this when it labors under the misconception that innocent people do not confess.

Given that the Miranda and interrogation reforms discussed in the previous two chapters are not likely to happen, allowing false confession experts to testify at trial may be the best way to prevent a defendant's false confession from turning into a wrongful conviction, and a wrongful conviction from turning into a prison sentence.

But this proposed legal reform, while realistic, is still hypothetical. The next chapter, therefore, takes us back into the interrogation room for something a bit more promising.

35

BYE-BYE REID?

There is another type of legal reform that is more than a mere possibility; it's actually underway in the real world. This reform involves making several changes to the way police interrogate their suspects.

Chapter 4 explained that interrogations are a guilt-presumptive process: the police aren't there to learn information, but rather to get the suspect to admit that he's guilty. Numerous other chapters in this book exposed the tactics that police use to reach that goal. For the most part, the police don't dream up these interrogation ploys on their own. Rather, they are formally trained in them. And the current and most popular method of this training is known as the Reid Technique.

"The dominant school of thought on interrogation tactics since the 1960s, distilled into a manual known as the Reid Technique, holds that detectives should relentlessly cajole their suspects toward their own set theory of the crime in question."[1] This approach "presumes the investigator has made no mistakes and can pressure their chosen perpetrator into a confession to match the investigator's narrative."[2] It also presumes that a confession is "an absolute sign of guilt," and that innocent people do not falsely confess.[3] This is a convenient presumption, of course, but one that has now been thoroughly debunked.

The good news is that change is afoot: "One of the nation's largest police consulting firms—one that has trained hundreds of thousands of cops from Chicago to New York and federal agents at almost every major agency—said it is tossing out the Reid technique because of the risk of false confessions."[4] The consulting firm, Wicklander-Zulawski & Associates, now recognizes that "[c]onfrontation is not an effective way of getting truthful information."[5]

To be sure, there is evidence to support the firm's decision to abandon confrontational and accusatorial interrogations. In addition to obvious examples like Brendan Dassey's case, there is also empirical evidence. In a 2014 meta-analysis of several field- and laboratory-based studies, the authors wrote:

> Field studies revealed that both information-gathering and accusatorial approaches were more likely to elicit a confession. . . . However, experimental studies revealed that the information-gathering approach preserved, and in some cases increased, the likelihood of *true* confessions, while simultaneously reducing the likelihood of *false* confessions. In contrast, the accusatorial approach increased both true *and* false confessions. . . . Conclusions: The available data support the effectiveness of an information-gathering style of interviewing suspects.[6]

The consulting firm's shift away from the Reid Method is, therefore, welcome news. However, there are still three potential roadblocks standing in the way of this current reform becoming a meaningful reform.

First, the obvious problem is that industry change moves at a snail's pace. "It will likely be years before Wicklander-Zulawski's thinking takes full root across the police training business, if history is any guide."[7]

Second, the consulting firm will be replacing Reid with "an approach it developed in-house—but the W-Z Method is a derivative of the Reid Technique itself."[8] That is, "the company is still training investigators to score confessions—just with a sunnier disposition and a slightly more open mind."[9] In short, "it's not immediately clear that its replacement will be better."[10]

And third, aside from all that, there is a much larger, underlying problem to be addressed: The presumption of guilt takes hold in the detective's mind long before the interrogation begins. It is therefore unlikely that a detective would be able to set that presumption aside and maintain "a slightly more open mind" when he begins to question his target. Instead, there needs to be a fundamental, psychological shift in the way that police investigate allegations from the get-go, before they enter the interrogation room.

To put it more bluntly, in many of the criminal cases I have defended, the term "police investigation" is a misnomer. Often, there is simply no investigation at all. Rather, the investigating officer simply rushes to judgment and then his tunnel vision leads him to collect only evidence that confirms his preexisting theory of the case. More specifically:

Tunnel vision is a natural human tendency that has particularly pernicious effects in the criminal justice system. . . . This process leads investigators, prosecutors, [and] judges . . . to focus on a particular conclusion and then filter all evidence in a case through the lens provided by that conclusion. Through that filter, all information supporting the adopted conclusion is elevated in significance, viewed as consistent with the other evidence, and deemed relevant and probative. Evidence inconsistent with the chosen theory is easily overlooked or dismissed as irrelevant, incredible, or unreliable.[11]

On the other hand, this type of quick-and-easy approach to law enforcement has at least two major benefits for the police. First, it conforms to society's view of justice in today's victim-centered culture where we are taught to believe the accuser and condemn the accused—all without knowing anything about the parties or the evidence. To question the truthfulness (or even the accuracy) of an accusation is frowned upon, as it supposedly marginalizes the "victim" and invalidates his or her experiences—or something to that effect.

The second benefit to rushing to judgment is that it saves the police a lot of time. If the police know what they want at the outset, they can find it more quickly and can also avoid getting sidetracked with anything that might contradict their theory of the case. In this way, policing is much like shopping for dinner. My trip to the grocery store will be much quicker and easier if I decide upfront that I want fast food, go straight to the frozen section, grab a premade extra-pepperoni pizza, and ignore the vegetables and fresh fish that might make me think about cooking a healthy dinner instead.

The drawback, of course, is that this type of tunnel vision and disregard for actual investigation can lead the police to target and arrest innocent people. I know this firsthand. While it is not always possible, in many cases I have been able to do incredibly simple things—things the police should have done—to establish my client's innocence. I am not referring to cases where I was able to negotiate a plea deal for a misdemeanor and a fine, or cases where I was able to go to trial and win an acquittal. I am instead referring to cases where I have all but proved my client's actual innocence before trial and the prosecutor therefore agreed to dismiss the case entirely.

This can be best illustrated by an example—subtle variations of which I see on a regular basis in my criminal defense practice. One of my former clients was charged with reckless endangerment of safety—a serious felony—for allegedly threatening another person and repeatedly (but unsuccessfully) thrusting a long box-cutter knife at the person's head. Like many of the criminal cases filed in Wisconsin, this one involved no actual injury to person or damage to property, and it was based solely on the word of the accuser.

As is their practice, the police blindly accepted the accuser's story— box-cutter knife and all—without learning anything about the parties or looking for any evidence that might contradict the allegation. I, however, was skeptical and was also interested in an alternative hypothesis. More to the point, I first wanted to know if the accuser had made any prior, inconsistent statements about what supposedly happened. I therefore obtained a copy of the accuser's 911 call—something the police could have easily done but failed to do—which went something like this:

Operator: This is 911, what is your emergency?

Caller: Yeah, Johnny Jones just threatened me, and I'm afraid! Please send the police! I want to file a complaint against him!

Operator: Okay, what did he do?

Caller: He said he was going to beat my ass! Hurry up! I'm afraid he might. He's done it before! He's hurt me before!

Operator: Okay, stay calm. Where is he now? And where are you?

Caller: He left, he drove off. I'm at 1212 Main Street.

Operator: Okay, are you hurt? Do you need a rescue squad?

Caller: No. He just threatened me; he didn't do anything this time.

Operator: I'm sending a squad car. *In case the police come in contact with him, I need to know if he has any weapons. Did Mr. Jones have anything like a knife or a gun or any type of weapon?*

Caller: *No, he didn't.*

Operator: The police are on the way. Stay inside and stay on the line with me until the police get there.

Caller: Okay. . . .

Operator: Alright, the police have arrived. They should be at your door any minute. Are they there yet?

Caller: Yeah, they just got here. Bye.

Within thirty seconds of hanging up the phone, the accuser then went on to tell the responding police officers the story of the box-cutter knife attack. Let's take a short multiple-choice test. Which of the following two options is more likely to be true?

A. Johnny Jones repeatedly thrust the box-cutter knife at the "victim's" head, but seconds later the "victim" forgot to mention this when the 911 operator specifically asked, "Did Mr. Jones have anything like a knife or a gun or any type of weapon?"

B. The 911 operator's question about whether "Mr. Jones [had] anything like a knife" is what gave the "victim" the idea for the story about the knife attack.

My money was on choice B. And with a little more investigation into my client's nonviolent background, as well as the accuser's real motive for wanting to get him arrested, I was able to spell out our defense for the prosecutor. The prosecutor then wisely and properly dismissed the criminal case before trial. And, to the prosecutor's credit, she did not try to squeeze a "disorderly conduct and a fine" out of my client; instead, she realized the "victim" was not a victim at all, but had trumped-up the allegation for other reasons—an all too common practice among those who take advantage of our victim-centered culture and use the police as their own personal tools.

If the investigating officer's tunnel vision was that bad that early in the case, just imagine how firmly the officer will be convinced of those beliefs by the time he gets Johnny Jones into the interrogation room. As a different investigating officer in another one of my cases explained (on camera) to a "victim": "Okay, we'll go find him, let him tell his side of the story, *and then arrest him.*" There's nothing like a foregone conclusion to start off an "investigation."

The larger point, of course, is this: implementing subtle change in how the police interrogate suspects is sort of like putting a fresh coat of paint on the top floor of a building with a rotting foundation. The problem runs much deeper, and such a superficial fix won't do much good. Unless the police are trained to keep an open mind early in a case, to be receptive to evidence that contradicts the accuser's story, and to actually take some basic steps to collect evidence regardless of where it might lead, changes in interrogation training are not likely to have any meaningful impact on reducing false confessions and wrongful convictions.

36

THE DANGERS OF DISCOURSE

This last chapter on legal reform is not exactly about a *legal* reform, but more about educational reform: We should consider educating young people—if not everyone—on the dangers of talking to government agents.

The police have done a great job of convincing us that they are our friends. For an example of this, we need only think back to Deputy Friendly from grade school. This type of early-age indoctrination has its benefits for the police. One is that it eventually creates a culture where people are more likely to trust the police and talk to them. And this remains true regardless of a suspect's age. As I explained in chapter 10, when I meet some of my adult clients, the first thing they do is express absolute disbelief that they have been arrested and charged with a crime. Why the surprise? Because, they tell me, "The detective seemed so nice, so honest. I thought he was on my side!"

There are times, to be sure, when law enforcement is on our side. But that's not always the case. Further, just because they're on our side one minute doesn't mean they'll be there the next. It is therefore important to understand some basic realities. To begin, and contrary to what the police tell their suspects to induce them to talk in the first place, it is very unlikely that what a suspect says can be used to help his defense at trial. And worse yet, there are countless ways in which what a suspect says can be used, either directly or indirectly, to convict him at trial. This is best illustrated with some concrete, real-life examples.

First, we saw in chapter 6 that the Miranda warning tells the suspect that anything he says can be used against him in court. When hearing this, most people rightly think that, if they admit to knowingly and intentionally committing a crime, their confession can be used to convict them of that crime. While this is certainly true, there are far more subtle ways that a prosecutor can use a suspect's statement to win a conviction.

One such way is that a suspect may admit secondary-level involvement, thinking that, if he paints himself as being less culpable than his co-actor, he is helping his own cause. Chapter 16 illustrated how Wiegert and Fassbender took advantage of—and probably even created—this misconception in Dassey by repeatedly urging him to blame Steven Avery. They told Dassey things like "he was telling you to do it," "he used you for this," "he threatened you," and—one of my personal favorites—"it's not your fault, he makes you do it." As Dassey later learned, however, being less culpable than Avery didn't serve as a successful trial defense. Instead, two or more defendants can be, and often are, convicted of the same crime.

Second, in cases where a suspect's statement is not recorded, the police, prosecutor, and judge can misquote the suspect or otherwise twist the statement into evidence of guilt. For an example of this, recall that DNA evidence eventually proved Steven Avery was innocent of the rape and attempted murder of Penny Beerntsen in the mid-1980s. However, Avery served eighteen years in prison before finally being exonerated. And one of the reasons he lost his case at the original jury trial and again on his appeal was that he talked to the police. In rejecting his request for a new trial, the Wisconsin Court of Appeals wrote:

> We also note that [Beerntsen's] identification of Avery was *corroborated by Avery's statements* at the time of his arrest. Although the testimony [at trial] indicated that the police told him only that he was under arrest "for attempted first degree murder," Avery told his wife [who was present at the time of his arrest] that "they say I murdered *a woman*" and asked [the police] where "*the lady*" lived. Since no one had mentioned the fact that the victim was a woman, the jury could properly deem Avery's statements to be inculpatory, corroborating the identification.[1]

Did Avery really say that, specifically? Maybe not. Maybe the arresting officers just heard what they wanted to hear, internalized it, and then repeated it on the witness stand at Avery's trial. On the other hand, maybe Avery did say that, in which case he would have an innocent explanation: he merely (and correctly) assumed that the victim was a woman, and his statement did not prove or even suggest that he committed the crime. (In fact, we now know beyond all doubt that he did not commit that crime.) If this is the case, then the police, prosecutor, and appellate court merely twisted Avery's words in pursuit of their goals: to obtain or affirm his conviction.

But regardless of the precise words Avery uttered, the lesson is painfully obvious: talking to the police did not help him and, instead, probably cost him dearly. (This, at least to me, makes it all the more baffling why so many members of Avery's family—including Dassey and Avery himself—were so willing to talk to law enforcement after Teresa Halbach went missing.)

Third, most interrogations today *are* recorded. Overall, this is a very good thing. But it also opens up entirely new ways for the government to use the suspect-turned-defendant's statement against him at trial. For example, in cases where the suspect denies guilt, the police love to shift the burden of proof to the suspect by asking him to prove his innocence. One common way to do this is simply to ask why "the victim" would make such an accusation if it were not true. Or, similarly, the police can present the suspect with evidence of his own guilt—whether real or fabricated— and then ask him to try to explain it away.

The problem is that the suspect often interprets these as good faith questions, as if the police are honestly searching for the truth and are looking for information that might prove the suspect's innocence. (As discussed earlier, however, an interrogation is a guilt-presumptive process, not a truth-seeking endeavor.) Thus, the suspect may play along and speculate about possible reasons why "the victim" would accuse him of a crime, or search his mind for ways to explain the physical evidence that the police are making up out of thin air.

What the suspect fails to realize, however, is that even though he is denying guilt, the prosecutor will later play this video-recorded interrogation for the jury. And at trial, the prosecutor will paint the defendant's earlier response to police questions as a ridiculous denial—nothing more than a guilty person's frantic attempt to create a frivolous defense. By comparison, this will make the prosecutor's case at trial seem even stronger. That is, when the jury looks at the two competing theories in the case, "if conviction of a crime fits the facts better than acquittal, it is extremely difficult to overcome the desire to match the facts with the *better* of the two models, *even if the [state's] case is not very strong.*"[2]

So much for the supposed burden of proof. In other words, when the defendant denies guilt and attempts to defend himself in the interrogation room, the prosecutor no longer has to prove his case beyond a reasonable doubt at trial. Rather—at least as a practical matter—the prosecutor just has to come up with a theory that sounds better than what the defendant cobbled together, off the top of his head, when facing the crushing pressure of the interrogation room.

Fourth, remember there are two parties to a police interrogation: the suspect and the police interrogator. And playing an interrogation video for the jury is a great way for the prosecutor to backdoor police testimony that he or she could never bring into court through the front door. By playing the interrogation video at trial—even when the video includes the defendant's adamant denial of guilt—the jury will hear the interrogator say things that he never would be allowed to say from the witness stand.

For example, it is well-settled law in Wisconsin (and in many other jurisdictions) that a witness in a trial may not testify that the defendant is lying when he denies guilt. Rather, the credibility of the defendant's testimony is an issue for the jury to decide. In Wisconsin, this is known as the Haseltine rule, which more generally prohibits one witness from vouching for another witness's testimony.[3] And it's a good rule, otherwise prosecutors would simply ask their police-detective witness whether they believe the defendant is lying, and the detective would invariably testify that he was. This is particularly dangerous given the common (but debunked) misconception that the police are trained as human lie detectors.[4]

But the interrogation video provides a backdoor for this forbidden testimony. At the time of the interrogation, the detective can call the defendant a liar as many times as he wants. Then, the prosecutor can play the video for the jury. In the Wisconsin case of *State v. Miller*, the defendant's appellate lawyer appealed a conviction that was obtained by such means:

> The main concern regarding vouching testimony is that it invades the jury's duty as the sole determiner of credibility. . . . Several times during [defendant] Miller's interview, Detective Primising stated that Mr. Miller was lying or not telling the truth. Moreover, there are numerous times during the interview when Mr. Miller would answer Detective Primising's questions and Detective Primising would state that Mr. Miller was lying or would insinuate that Mr. Miller was lying. The interview was played before the jury and received as evidence during the trial. Detective Primising's opinion as to whether Mr. Miller was telling the truth during the interview is a clear violation of Haseltine. *It makes little difference that Detective Primising did not directly testify whether he believed Mr. Miller was telling the truth during the interview. The effect on the jury was the same or possibly even worse.*[5]

The defendant's appellate lawyer is correct. Nonetheless, the court saw the opportunity to affirm the defendant's conviction by drawing a meaningless distinction: "As the trial court observed, Primising's statements amounted to an unsworn 'interrogation technique.'"[6] The court therefore held that, "because Primising's statements were not made as sworn testimony . . . but were instead made in the context of a pretrial police investigation, the Haseltine rule was not violated and the trial court did not err by permitting the DVD to be played for the jury."[7]

Of course, if the defendant had declined to speak to the detective—and instead exercised his right to remain silent or to consult with a lawyer—the detective's opinions about the defendant's untruthfulness could not have been sneaked into court through the backdoor (the interrogation video) and, therefore, never would have reached the jury.

Finally, even when the suspect denies guilt, and even when the interrogation was recorded to prevent the interrogators from misquoting the suspect, there are still risks. And to illustrate this final point of the chapter, we can now return to Dassey's jury trial where the government's spin machine was operating at high speed.

Recall from chapter 4 that on November 6, 2005, just after Teresa Halbach went missing, Detectives O'Neill and Baldwin got their hooks into Dassey and interrogated him in the back of a squad car. Dassey did not say anything incriminating in that interrogation. Nonetheless, the audio-recorded statement was used against him at trial—not for its content, but so one of the interrogators, Detective O'Neill, could wax eloquent about Dassey's "demeanor" during their exchange. He testified:

> Ah, I interview a lot of people, and, ah, Mr. Dassey's demeanor was, ah, *different*. When it came to specifics regarding Teresa Halbach, Steven Avery, what happened on that day, he'd sit there, head down, withdrawn, motionless, it was ah, ah, a demeanor that I felt, from all the years of training and experience that I've had in dealing with people, an inner struggle, a conflict, *he was hiding something*. It was not gonna be a ten minute interview as to what he saw. There was something more.[8]

The detective admitted on cross-examination that he was not trained as a child psychologist or even as a psychologist, that he had never seen Dassey before that day and had no idea how he reacts to stressful situations or to authority figures, and that he wrote nothing about Dassey's allegedly "different" demeanor in his police report. Rather, he was testifying based on his alleged memory of a short interrogation that occurred *sixteen months earlier*.[9]

Further, O'Neill testified that Dassey struck him as someone who was "hiding something," yet no one bothered Dassey for a substantive follow-up interrogation until Wiegert and Fassbender pulled him from his class nearly four months later. And that decision, Wiegert said, was made based on a child relative's opinion that Dassey had lost weight and was behaving differently since Halbach's disappearance.

One hopes that jurors are able to see through this sort of government sophistry that the prosecutor and Detective O'Neill were concocting at trial, but that all depends on the individual jurors' critical faculties. Nonetheless, the stark reality is that, in Dassey's case and in all of the examples discussed above, the defendant's decision to talk to the police did not help, but instead probably did significant damage.

If we want to educate people on these types of dangers, we would be wise to look to two sources. One source is the Miranda warning itself. Despite its numerous gaps and flaws, it does make one thing clear: *anything* you say can and will be used against you in court. Further, we can include the warning that, in addition to *what* you say, *how* you say it can also be spun or twisted into evidence of your guilt.

As we learned in earlier chapters, though, the police don't have to read a suspect the Miranda warning unless the police have *arrested* the suspect and intend to question him. Therefore, it would also be wise to remember the unnecessary but accurate warning Fassbender uttered to Dassey before questioning him at Mishicot High School: "Um, you're not under arrest, you know that. You're free to go at anytime you want. Ah, just listen to us, you don't have to answer any questions if you don't want to and stuff like that, OK?"[10]

Had Dassey said, "Okay, I don't want to answer any questions and I'm going back to class," or "Okay, then I'd like to have my mom or a lawyer present before going any further," he could have avoided being charged, tried, convicted, and imprisoned—all without an eyewitness, a piece of physical evidence, or even an accusation linking him to the crime.

While on the topic of imprisonment, let's turn next to the book's final section to see what has been happening with Dassey's case.

Part VII
POSTSCRIPT

37

CALLING THE SUPREME COURT

"I'll take my case all the way to the Supreme Court!"

That phrase has been uttered by countless people ranging from disgruntled losers in small claims court all the way up to huge corporate litigants in federal courts of appeal. But the reality is that it's incredibly difficult to convince the Supreme Court of the United States to actually hear any given case. Nonetheless, and against all odds, Dassey's appellate lawyers are trying.

After this book was completed but before it went to press, Dassey's appellate team—which has now reached a total of ten lawyers located in five different states and Washington D.C.—filed a lengthy petition for a writ of certiorari with the Court.[1] In it, they ask the Court to accept Dassey's case for review, and they've highlighted several selling points. First, they illustrated how Wiegert and Fassbender used egregious interrogation tactics to take advantage of Dassey's deficiencies and coerce a confession. They capped-off this lengthy analysis as follows:

> Put simply, the interrogators took advantage of Dassey's youth and mental limitations to convince him they were on his side, ignored his manifest inability to correctly answer many of their questions about the crimes, fed him facts so he could say what they wanted to hear, and promised that he would be set free if he did so. The resulting confession was more theirs than his. Extracted through the use of psychologically coercive tactics leveraged against his personal vulnerabilities, it was assuredly not the product of Dassey's free will. As Dassey himself said to his mother just moments after the interrogation ended: "They got to my head."[2]

Second, they explained why the state appellate court's two-paragraph recitation of some cherry-picked facts, along with its citation of only a portion of the applicable legal standard, falls short of what the law demands. In other words, to use the language of the AEDPA discussed in earlier chapters, the state court's decision was not *merely* wrong, but *so* wrong that it must be reversed. "The state court utterly failed, as part of its totality-of-the-circumstances analysis, to afford Dassey's confession the 'special care' this Court requires for juvenile confessions."[3]

More specifically, "just *listing* a defendant's particular characteristics" does not pass the test.[4] Nor is it adequate merely to "jump to the conclusion that the confession was voluntary."[5] Instead, actual legal analysis—the very thing for which Wisconsin's appellate court judges are grossly overpaid—is required. And when analyzing the facts and circumstances, "not every circumstance is equally important."[6] For example, "the upholstery on the couch Dassey sat on" during the interrogation is simply not as important as Dassey's mental limitations and Wiegert and Fassbender's dozens of threats and false promises of leniency.[7]

The appellate team also sold the Court on the national significance of this case—a case that isn't just about Brendan Dassey. Rather, coercive interrogation tactics are widespread, and the false confessions they produce are a nationwide problem. Worse yet, state courts are ignoring binding Supreme Court precedent and are instead rubberstamping convictions—even when prosecutors win those convictions by using obviously coerced confessions. The Court therefore needs to remind these lower courts of the importance of stare decisis, or their duty to follow binding precedent.

> The Wisconsin Court of Appeals' departure from this Court's precedent is no isolated incident. Since this Court decided *Gallegos*, *Gault*, and *Fare*, lower courts have often failed to follow those decisions. The consequences of those failures have been illustrated not only by research demonstrating how vulnerable juveniles and intellectually disabled persons are to police interrogation tactics, but also by data on wrongful convictions resulting from false confessions. Certiorari is warranted here not only to reaffirm this Court's holdings (and lower courts' obligation to follow them), but also to provide guidance on how to apply those holdings so as to minimize false confessions—which not only lead to innocent people being jailed but also leave the perpetrators free to victimize others.[8]

Will the Supreme Court be persuaded to hear Dassey's appeal? The odds are certainly against it. However, in a bizarre, rollercoaster case like this—a case with unbelievable facts, an obviously coerced (and false) confession, unparalleled national (and even international) popularity, and a very unusual procedural history—it's difficult to rule out the possibility. In other words, the case certainly has an "anything could happen" aura about it.

On the other hand, if the Supreme Court refuses to hear Dassey's case, this much is certain: the interrogation and conviction of Brendan Dassey will go down as one of the greatest injustices in the history of American criminal law.

NOTES

Chapter 1

1. The interrogation transcripts include errors and informal diction by the speakers, such as the interrogators' frequent use of "ta" in place of the word "to." I have preserved most of these errors for the purpose of authenticity. In addition, however, there are transcription errors, including misspelled words and omitted punctuation marks. I have taken the liberty of correcting obvious transcription errors to improve readability. Toward this end, the ellipses (. . .) used in this book indicate that material in a transcript has been omitted from the quotation; ellipses that appeared in the original transcripts are typically ignored. Also for the purpose of readability, I sometimes changed a capital letter to lowercase, and vice versa, without using brackets. Readers can find the original transcripts of Dassey's interrogations at http://www.stevenaverycase.org/police-interviews-and-interrogations/.

2. This version paraphrases Ken Kratz's opening statement in Dassey's jury trial and also incorporates some additional elements from the interrogation transcripts. Ken Kratz's pretrial press conference, where he rendered the now-famous dramatic reading of the alleged confession, is discussed in chapter 21.

3. For a parody of Ken Kratz's overly dramatic press conference where he overused the word "sweat" or some variation thereof, see Axilrod, *Ken Kratz Press Conference—Extra Sweaty Edition* (January 19, 2016), at https://www.youtube.com/watch?v=TzgBgceapmA.

Chapter 2

1. *State v. Jerrell C.J.*, 283 Wis.2d 145, 171 (2005).

2. A defendant's prior record can be used against him at trial in several different ways. For example, the mere fact of a prior conviction can often be used to impeach the defendant's credibility if he or she testifies at trial. The details of a prior conviction may be used at trial regardless of whether the defendant testifies simply to demonstrate his or her motive to commit the charged crime or to prove his or her identity as the perpetrator of the charged crime, for example. See Michael D. Cicchini and Lawrence T. White, "Convictions Based on Character: An

Empirical Test of Other-Acts Evidence," *Florida Law Review* 70 (2018), which discusses multiple ways that a defendant's prior convictions can be used at trial.

3. *Jerrell C.J.*, 152–53.

4. Ibid., 155 (quoting the earlier court of appeals' decision in the case) (emphasis added).

5. Ibid., 167.

6. Ibid., 168.

7. Ibid., 173.

8. Ibid., 169.

9. Ibid., 171.

10. Wis. Stats. § 968.073. This statute requires law enforcement to make an audio or audiovisual recording of *custodial* interrogations where the interrogator suspects that the suspect committed a *felony*. However, even for that narrow class of interrogations, there are several exceptions to the recording requirement, including when the failure to make such a recording was in "good faith" (Wis. Stats. § 972.115). Even if none of the good faith exceptions apply, the failure to record an interrogation does not mean the defendant's statement is suppressed or excluded from evidence at trial. The most the defendant would be entitled to is a jury instruction that Wisconsin's policy is to record the interrogation, but law enforcement failed to do so, and the jury may consider that when evaluating the evidence.

Chapter 3

1. James R. Agar II, "The Admissibility of False Confession Expert Testimony," *Army Lawyer* 26 (1999).

2. Evan Nesterak, "Coerced to Confess: The Psychology of False Confessions," *The Psych Report* (October 21, 2014), at http://thepsychreport.com/conversations/coerced-to-confess-the-psychology-of-false-confessions/.

3. Ibid.

4. "False Confessions: From Awareness to Reform: Facts and Figures," *False Confessions*, at http://www.falseconfessions.org/fact-a-figures (accessed May 13, 2017).

5. Danielle E. Chojnacki, Michael D. Cicchini, and Lawrence T. White, "An Empirical Basis for the Admission of Expert Testimony on False Confessions," *Arizona State Law Journal* 40, no. 1 (2008): 4–6.

6. *Making a Murderer*, dir. Moira Demos and Laura Ricciardi, aired December 18, 2015 (Los Angeles: Synthesis Films and Netflix).

7. Melissa B. Russano et al., "Investigating True and False Confessions Within a Novel Experimental Paradigm," *Psychological Science* 16, no. 6 (2005): 483–85.

8. Wis. Stats. § 941.30 (2) ("Whoever recklessly endangers another's safety is guilty of a Class G felony.").

9. Christine Wiseman and Michael Tobin, *Wisconsin Practice Series: Criminal Practice & Procedure* § 15.6, second edition (Eagan, MN: West, 2008) ("[T]he Wisconsin Supreme Court has concluded that where the crime is against persons rather than property, there are, as a general rule, as many offenses as individuals affected.").

10. Wis. Stats. § 939.50 (3) (g) ("Penalties for felonies are as follows. . . . For a Class G felony, a fine not to exceed $25,000 or imprisonment not to exceed 10 years, or both.").

11. Wis. Stats. § 973.15 (2) ("[T]he court may impose as many sentences as there are convictions and may provide that any such sentence be . . . consecutive to any other sentence imposed at the same time or previously.").

Chapter 4

1. Louise Chang, "John Mark Karr and the False Confession: Why?," *WebMD Mental Health* (August 29, 2006), at http://www.webmd.com/mental-health/features/john-mark-karr-false-confession-why#1.

2. Ibid.

3. Ibid.

4. Interrogation of Brendan Dassey, Marinette County Squad Car (Nov. 6, 2005), 19–20 (emphasis added), at http://www.stevenaverycase.org/wp-content/uploads/2016/03/Brendan-Dassey-Interview-Transcript-2005Nov06.pdf.

5. Ibid., 20–23 (emphasis added).

6. Danielle Chojnacki, Michael D. Cicchini, and Lawrence T. White, "An Empirical Basis for the Admission of Expert Testimony on False Confessions," *Arizona State Law Journal* 40, no. 1 (2008): 3.

7. Ibid.

8. Trial Transcript Day 4, *State v. Dassey*, Case No. 06-CF-88, Manitowoc County, Wis. (April 19, 2007), 189, at http://www.stevenaverycase.org/wp-content/uploads/2017/02/Dassey-Trial-Transcripts.pdf.

9. Ibid., 198–99.

10. Ibid.

11. Trial Transcript Day 5, *State v. Dassey*, Case No. 06-CF-88, Manitowoc County, Wis. (April 20, 2007), 5, at http://www.stevenaverycase.org/wp-content/uploads/2017/02/Dassey-Trial-Transcripts.pdf.

12. Interrogation of Brendan Dassey, Mishicot High School (Feb. 27, 2006), 443, at http://www.stevenaverycase.org/wp-content/uploads/2016/02/Brendan-Dassey-Interview-at-School-Transcript-2006Feb27_text.pdf.

13. Ibid., 447.

14. Chojnacki et al., "An Empirical Basis," 19.

Chapter 5

1. Interrogation of Brendan Dassey, Manitowoc County Sheriff's Dept. (Mar. 1, 2006), 527, at http://www.stevenaverycase.org/wp-content/uploads/2016/02/Brendan-Dassey-Interview-Transcript-2006Mar01_text.pdf.

2. Ibid., 547.

3. Interrogation of Brendan Dassey, Marinette County Squad Car (Nov. 6, 2005), 22, at http://www.stevenaverycase.org/wp-content/uploads/2016/03/Brendan-Dassey-Interview-Transcript-2005Nov06.pdf.

4. Ibid., 26 (emphasis added).

5. Interrogation of Brendan Dassey, Mishicot High School (Feb. 27, 2006), 464, at http://www.stevenaverycase.org/wp-content/uploads/2016/02/Brendan-Dassey-Interview-at-School-Transcript-2006Feb27_text.pdf.

6. Danielle Chojnacki, Michael D. Cicchini, and Lawrence T. White, "An Empirical Basis for the Admission of Expert Testimony on False Confessions," *Arizona State Law Journal* 40, no. 1 (2008): 17.

7. Saul M. Kassin et al., "Police Interviewing and Interrogation: A Self-Report Survey of Police Practices and Beliefs," *Law & Human Behavior* 31 (2007): 391 (62 percent of interrogators reported that they "always" isolate the suspect "away from family and friends.").

8. Marinette County Sheriff's Department Supplemental Report Investigative Division, Case No. 05-4120 (Jan. 31, 2016), 1 (discussing Dassey's interrogation in the squad car on November 6, 2005), at http://www.stevenaverycase.org/wp-content/uploads/2016/01/Brendan-Dassey-Interview-Report-2005Nov06.pdf.

9. Interrogation of Brendan Dassey, Marinette County Squad Car, 36 (emphasis added).

10. Brief of Defendant-Appellant, *State v. Dassey*, 2010AP3105-CR (Wis. Ct. App., Dec. 1, 2011), 82–83 (internal citations to the record omitted).

Chapter 6

1. Interrogation of Brendan Dassey, Mishicot High School (Feb. 27, 2006), 440, at http://www.stevenaverycase.org/wp-content/uploads/2016/02/Brendan-Dassey-Interview-at-School-Transcript-2006Feb27_text.pdf.

2. Ibid., 442 (emphasis added).

3. Ibid., 443.

4. Ibid., 441.

5. Ibid., 443–44.

6. Anthony Domanico, Michael D. Cicchini, and Lawrence T. White, "Overcoming Miranda: A Content Analysis of the Miranda Portion of Police Interrogations," *Idaho Law Review* 49, no. 1 (2012): 2 (emphasis added).

7. 384 U.S. 436 (1966).

8. Domanico et al., "Overcoming Miranda," 2.

9. Ibid., 2–3 (analyzing and testing the Miranda warning used by the police department in Milwaukee, Wisconsin).

10. Charles J. Ogletree, "Are Confessions Really Good for the Soul? A Proposal to Mirandize Miranda," *Harvard Law Review* 100 (1987): 1828 (The police "have little interest in protecting the suspect's rights. . . . Their objective is to obtain a confession.").

11. Ibid.

Chapter 7

1. *United States v. Yusuff*, 96 F.3d 982, 987 (7th Cir. 1996). The court stated, "In order to protect an individual's right against self-incrimination under the Fifth Amendment, the Supreme Court held in *Miranda v. Arizona*, 384 U.S. 436, 444 (1966), that suspects must be advised of certain rights before they are subjected to 'custodial interrogation.' A suspect must be both in custody and subject to 'interrogation' to trigger the Miranda warnings requirement."

2. 193 N.W.2d 711 (Wis. 1972).

3. Michael D. Cicchini, "The New Miranda Warning," *Southern Methodist University Law Review* 65 (2012): 911, 926–27.

4. *McClellan v. State*, 193 N.W.2d 711, 716-17 (Wis. 1972).

5. Interrogation of Brendan Dassey, Mishicot High School (Feb. 27, 2006), 440, at http://www.stevenaverycase.org/wp-content/uploads/2016/02/Brendan-Dassey-Interview-at-School-Transcript-2006Feb27_text.pdf.

6. Ibid.

7. Ibid., 443–44.

8. Ibid., 447.

9. Ibid., 449.

Chapter 8

1. At least three studies found that approximately 80 percent of suspects waived their Miranda rights. See Paul Softley, *Police Interrogation: An Observational Study in Four Police Stations*, Home Office Research Unit Report (London: HMSO, 1980), 29; Richard A. Leo, "Inside the Interrogation Room," *Journal of Criminal Law & Criminology* 86 (1996): 276; Paul G. Cassell and Bret S. Hayman, "Police Interrogation in the 1990s: An Empirical Study of the Effects of Miranda," *UCLA Law Review* 43 (1996): 859.

2. Anthony Domanico, Michael D. Cicchini, and Lawrence T. White, "Overcoming Miranda: A Content Analysis of the Miranda Portion of Police Interrogations," *Idaho Law Review* 49, no. 1 (2012): 2.

3. Ibid., 14. Psychologists and others can measure readability of language by using the "Flesch-Kincaid readability" test.

4. Ibid., 15–16 (emphasis added).

5. Interrogation of Brendan Dassey, Two Rivers Police Dept. (Feb. 27, 2006), 484 (emphasis added), at http://www.stevenaverycase.org/wp-content/uploads/2016/02/Brendan-Dassey-Interview-at-Station-Transcript-2006Feb27_text.pdf.

6. Domanico et al., "Overcoming Miranda," 17. More specifically, "Comprehension degrades in part because, when someone speaks more rapidly, there are changes in vocal inflection and intensity, as well as changes in the relative duration of consonants, vowels, and pauses."

7. Ibid. (emphasis added).

8. Ibid.

9. Interrogation of Brendan Dassey, Manitowoc County Sheriff's Dept. (Mar. 1, 2006), 526, at http://www.stevenaverycase.org/wp-content/uploads/2016/02/Brendan-Dassey-Interview-Transcript-2006Mar01_text.pdf. The audio recording of the interrogation demonstrates that Wiegert delivered his seventy-seven-word Miranda spiel in approximately seventeen seconds, which translates to nearly 272 words per minute.

10. Ibid.

11. Interrogation of Brendan Dassey, Two Rivers Police Dept., 484 (emphasis added).

12. Ibid.

13. Prosecutors still find (illegal) ways to use a defendant's *post*-Miranda silence at trial. For example, they sometimes have police officers sneakily testify that they "*tried* to get a statement from the defendant," thereby communicating that the defendant exercised the right to remain silent. While this is clearly illegal, courts often view it as harmless error when defendants later challenge their guilty verdicts on appeal. And in a related matter, the admissibility at trial of a defendant's *pre*-Miranda silence as evidence of guilt is a much trickier subject. See Sandra Guerra Thompson, "Evading Miranda: How Seibert and Patane Failed to "Save" Miranda," *Valparaiso University Law Review* 40 (2006): 647.

14. Interrogation of Brendan Dassey, Two Rivers Police Dept., 484.

15. Ibid.

16. Ibid. (emphasis added).

17. Ibid.

Chapter 9

1. Marcy Strauss, "The Sounds of Silence: Reconsidering the Invocation of the Right to Remain Silent under Miranda," *William & Mary Bill of Rights Journal* 17 (2009): 822.

2. Anthony Domanico, Michael D. Cicchini, and Lawrence T. White, "Overcoming Miranda: A Content Analysis of the Miranda Portion of Police Interrogations," Idaho Law Review 49, no. 1 (2012): 14.

3. Ibid., 15.

4. Interrogation of Brendan Dassey, Two Rivers Police Dept. (Feb. 27, 2006), 484, at http://www.stevenaverycase.org/wp-content/uploads/2016/02/Brendan-Dassey-Interview-at-Station-Transcript-2006Feb27_text.pdf.

5. Interrogation of Brendan Dassey, Manitowoc County Sheriff's Dept. (Mar. 1, 2006), 539, at http://www.stevenaverycase.org/wp-content/uploads/2016/02/Brendan-Dassey-Interview-Transcript-2006Mar01_text.pdf.

6. Interrogation of Brendan Dassey, Mishicot High School (Feb. 27, 2006), 443 (emphasis added), at http://www.stevenaverycase.org/wp-content/uploads/2016/02/Brendan-Dassey-Interview-at-School-Transcript-2006Feb27_text.pdf.

7. Ibid., 451.

8. Interrogation of Brendan Dassey, Manitowoc County Sheriff's Dept., 540.

9. Ibid.

10. Ibid.

11. Interrogation of Brendan Dassey, Mishicot High School, 467 (emphasis added).

12. Ibid., 446.

13. Interrogation of Brendan Dassey, Manitowoc County Sheriff's Dept., 541 (emphasis added).

14. Interrogation of Brendan Dassey, Mishicot High School, 453 (emphasis added).

15. *State v. Saeger*, 2010 WI App 135, ¶ 3 (emphasis added) (ellipses omitted).

16. Ibid., 11. Courts are willing to twist plain language beyond belief in order to find that defendants did not properly invoke their right to remain silent or their right to counsel. See Michael D. Cicchini, "The New Miranda Warning," *Southern Methodist University Law Review* 65, (2012), 917–20, 922–25 (collecting cases where defendants' clear invocations of their rights were found to be ambiguous and therefore insufficient to actually invoke those rights).

Chapter 10

1. Interrogation of Brendan Dassey, Manitowoc County Sheriff's Dept. (Mar. 1, 2006), 547, at http://www.stevenaverycase.org/wp-content/uploads/2016/02/Brendan-Dassey-Interview-Transcript-2006Mar01_text.pdf.

2. Charles D. Weisselberg, "Mourning Miranda," *California Law Review* 96 (2008): 1562 (emphasis added).

3. Anthony Domanico, Michael D. Cicchini, and Lawrence T. White, "Overcoming Miranda: A Content Analysis of the Miranda Portion of Police Interrogations," *Idaho Law Review* 49, no. 1 (2012): 16.

4. Interrogation of Brendan Dassey, Manitowoc County Sheriff's Dept., 533.

5. Ibid., 539.

6. Interrogation of Brendan Dassey, Mishicot High School (Feb. 27, 2006), 440, at http://www.stevenaverycase.org/wp-content/uploads/2016/02/Brendan-Dassey-Interview-at-School-Transcript-2006Feb27_text.pdf.

7. Ibid., 443.

8. Ibid., 441.

9. Interrogation of Brendan Dassey, Manitowoc County Sheriff's Dept., 531–32.

10. Ibid., 534.

11. Ibid., 532.

12. Ibid.

13. Ibid., 529.

14. Ibid.

15. Ibid., 530.

16. Ibid., 535.

17. Ibid., 533.

Chapter 11

1. Saul M. Kassin and Karlyn McNall, "Police Interrogations and Confessions: Communicating Promises and Threats by Pragmatic Implication," *Law & Human Behavior* 15 (1991): 234–35 (parenthetical omitted).

2. Interrogation of Brendan Dassey, Marinette County Squad Car (Nov. 6, 2005), at http://www.stevenaverycase.org/wp-content/uploads/2016/03/Brendan-Dassey-Interview-Transcript-2005Nov06.pdf.

3. Trial Transcript Day 4, *State v. Dassey*, Case No. 06-CF-88, Manitowoc County, Wis. (April 19, 2007), 198–99, at http://www.stevenaverycase.org/wp-content/uploads/2017/02/Dassey-Trial-Transcripts.pdf.

4. Wis. Stats. § 946.41 ("[W]hoever knowingly . . . obstructs an officer while such officer is doing any act in an official capacity and with lawful authority is guilty of a Class A misdemeanor. . . . 'Obstructs' includes without limitation knowingly giving false information to the officer . . ."). Dassey, however, was a juvenile and may have been the subject of juvenile proceedings, rather than a criminal case, if there was a basis for an allegation of obstructing.

5. Kassin and McNall "Police Interrogations and Confessions," 234–35.

6. Interrogation of Brendan Dassey, Mishicot High School (Feb. 27, 2006), 442 (emphasis added), at http://www.stevenaverycase.org/wp-content/uploads/2016/02/Brendan-Dassey-Interview-at-School-Transcript-2006Feb27_text.pdf.

7. Kassin and McNall, "Police Interrogations and Confessions," 234–35.

8. Interrogation of Brendan Dassey, Mishicot High School, 442.

9. Ibid., 443.

10. Ibid., 447.

11. Interrogation of Brendan Dassey, Marinette County Squad Car, 22.

12. Danielle E. Chojnacki, Michael D. Cicchini, and Lawrence T. White, "An Empirical Basis for the Admission of Expert Testimony on False Confessions," *Arizona State Law Journal* 40, no. 1 (2008): 16.

13. Ibid., 18.

Chapter 12

1. *United States v. Rutledge*, 900 F.2d 1127, 1129 (7th Cir. 1990). Courts do not take the language "free and voluntary" too seriously, however. "Taken seriously it would require the exclusion of virtually all fruits of custodial interrogation, since few choices to confess can be thought truly 'free' when made by a person who is incarcerated and is being questioned by armed officers without the presence of counsel or anyone else to give him moral support. The formula is not

taken seriously. . . . In any event, very few incriminating statements, custodial or otherwise, are held to be involuntary, though few are the product of a choice that the interrogators left completely free."

2. Ibid.

3. Interrogation of Brendan Dassey, Manitowoc County Sheriff's Dept. (Mar. 1, 2006), 541, at http://www.stevenaverycase.org/wp-content/uploads/2016/02/Brendan-Dassey-Interview-Transcript-2006Mar01_text.pdf.

4. *State v. Deets*, 187 Wis. 2d 630, 636 (Ct. App. 1994).

5. Interrogation of Brendan Dassey, Mishicot High School (Feb. 27, 2006), 442, at http://www.stevenaverycase.org/wp-content/uploads/2016/02/Brendan-Dassey-Interview-at-School-Transcript-2006Feb27_text.pdf.

6. Ibid.

7. Ibid., 447.

8. Ibid., 446.

9. Ibid., 448 (emphasis added).

10. Interrogation of Brendan Dassey, Manitowoc County Sheriff's Dept., 547 (emphasis added).

11. Ibid., 541 (emphasis added).

12. Brief of Petitioner-Appellee Brendan Dassey, *Dassey v. Dittmann*, No. 16-3397 (U.S. Ct. App. 7th Cir., Dec. 6, 2016), 36 (emphasis original).

13. Ibid., 35–36 (internal citations and ellipses within quotations omitted).

14. Brief of Defendant-Appellant, *State v. Dassey*, 2010AP3105-CR (Wis. Ct. App., Dec. 1, 2011), 85 (internal citations to the record omitted).

15. Ibid.

16. Interrogation of Brendan Dassey, Manitowoc County Sheriff's Dept., 613.

Chapter 13

1. 837 N.W.2d 178 (Wis. Ct. App. 2013).

2. Ibid., ¶ 3 (emphasis added).

3. Ibid., ¶ 3, footnote 2.

4. For further discussion of this case, see Michael D. Cicchini, "The Non-Recommendation Recommendation (and Other Government Bullshit)," *The Legal Watchdog* (August 17, 2013), at http://thelegalwatchdog.blogspot.com/2013/08/the-non-recommendation-recommendation.html. This "non-recommendation recommendation" argument is the type of prosecutorial sophistry we defense lawyers must combat on a regular basis. Such reasoning wouldn't earn a passing grade in a college-level class in informal logic, yet is routinely tolerated in the courtroom. For examples of slightly more sophisticated sophistry in the context

of jury trials, see Michael D. Cicchini, "Combating Prosecutor Misconduct in Closing Arguments," *Oklahoma Law Review* 70 (2018).

5. *Making a Murderer*, dir. Moira Demos and Laura Ricciardi, aired December 18, 2015 (Los Angeles: Synthesis Films and Netflix).

6. Interrogation of Brendan Dassey, Mishicot High School (Feb. 27, 2006), 448, at http://www.stevenaverycase.org/wp-content/uploads/2016/02/Brendan-Dassey-Interview-at-School-Transcript-2006Feb27_text.pdf.

7. Interrogation of Brendan Dassey, Manitowoc County Sheriff's Dept. (Mar. 1, 2006), 541, at http://www.stevenaverycase.org/wp-content/uploads/2016/02/Brendan-Dassey-Interview-Transcript-2006Mar01_text.pdf.

8. Interrogation of Brendan Dassey, Mishicot High School, 442.

9. Ibid., 443.

10. Interrogation of Brendan Dassey, Manitowoc County Sheriff's Dept., 547.

11. Ibid.

12. Ibid.

13. Ibid. (emphasis added).

14. Ibid.

15. Interrogation of Brendan Dassey, Marinette County Squad Car (Nov. 6, 2005), 23–25 (emphasis added), at http://www.stevenaverycase.org/wp-content/uploads/2016/03/Brendan-Dassey-Interview-Transcript-2005Nov06.pdf.

Chapter 14

1. Brief of Petitioner-Appellee Brendan Dassey, *Dassey v. Dittmann*, No. 16-3397 (U.S. Ct. App. 7th Cir., Dec. 6, 2016), 5 (emphasis added) (internal quotations, citations, and ellipses omitted).

2. Interrogation of Brendan Dassey, Manitowoc County Sheriff's Dept. (Mar. 1, 2006), 584–87 (emphasis added), at http://www.stevenaverycase.org/wp-content/uploads/2016/02/Brendan-Dassey-Interview-Transcript-2006Mar01_text.pdf.

3. Ibid., 615 (emphasis added).

4. Ibid. (emphasis added).

5. Ibid., 601–2.

6. Ibid., 603.

7. Interrogation of Brendan Dassey, Mishicot High School (Feb. 27, 2006), 451, at http://www.stevenaverycase.org/wp-content/uploads/2016/02/Brendan-Dassey-Interview-at-School-Transcript-2006Feb27_text.pdf.

Chapter 15

1. Trial Transcript Day 5, *State v. Dassey*, Case No. 06-CF-88, Manitowoc County, Wis. (April 20, 2007), 11 (emphasis added), at http://www.stevenavery-case.org/wp-content/uploads/2017/02/Dassey-Trial-Transcripts.pdf.

2. Brief of Petitioner-Appellee Brendan Dassey, *Dassey v. Dittmann*, No. 16-3397 (U.S. Ct. App. 7th Cir., Dec. 6, 2016), 38 (internal quotations and citations omitted).

3. Ibid., 39.

4. Ibid. (emphasis added).

5. Interrogation of Brendan Dassey, Mishicot High School (Feb. 27, 2006), 441–42, at http://www.stevenaverycase.org/wp-content/uploads/2016/02/Brendan-Dassey-Interview-at-School-Transcript-2006Feb27_text.pdf.

6. Ibid., 443.

7. Ibid., 447–48.

8. Ibid., 449.

9. Ibid., 451–52.

10. Ibid., 452–53.

11. Ibid., 453.

12. Interrogation of Brendan Dassey, Manitowoc County Sheriff's Dept. (Mar. 1, 2006), 541, at http://www.stevenaverycase.org/wp-content/uploads/2016/02/Brendan-Dassey-Interview-Transcript-2006Mar01_text.pdf.

13. Ibid., 552–53.

14. Interrogation of Brendan Dassey, Mishicot High School (Feb. 27, 2006), 461–62.

15. Interrogation of Brendan Dassey, Two Rivers Police Dept. (Feb. 27, 2006), 495–96, at http://www.stevenaverycase.org/wp-content/uploads/2016/02/Brendan-Dassey-Interview-at-Station-Transcript-2006Feb27_text.pdf.

16. Interrogation of Brendan Dassey, Manitowoc County Sheriff's Dept. (Mar. 1, 2006), 560.

17. Ibid., 561.

18. Ibid., 565–66 (emphasis added).

19. Ibid., 571.

20. Ibid.

21. Ibid.

22. Ibid.

23. Ibid., 572

24. Ibid., 580–81.

25. Ibid., 587.

Chapter 16

1. Saul M. Kassin, "The Psychology of Confession Evidence," *American Psychologist* 52 (1997): 223.

2. Danielle Chojnacki, Michael D. Cicchini, and Lawrence T. White, "An Empirical Basis for the Admission of Expert Testimony on False Confessions," *Arizona State Law Journal* 40, no. 1 (2008): 18 (emphasis original) (citing Melissa B. Russano et al., "Investigating True and False Confessions within a Novel Experimental Paradigm," *Psychological Science* 16 [2005]: 483–85).

3. Interrogation of Brendan Dassey, Mishicot High School (Feb. 27, 2006), 442, at http://www.stevenaverycase.org/wp-content/uploads/2016/02/Brendan-Dassey-Interview-at-School-Transcript-2006Feb27_text.pdf.

4. Ibid.

5. Ibid., 453.

6. Ibid.

7. Interrogation of Brendan Dassey, Manitowoc County Sheriff's Dept. (Mar. 1, 2006), 552, at http://www.stevenaverycase.org/wp-content/uploads/2016/02/Brendan-Dassey-Interview-Transcript-2006Mar01_text.pdf.

8. Ibid., 555.

9. Ibid., 574.

10. Ibid.

11. Ibid., 584.

12. Ibid.

13. Ibid., 585.

14. Ibid., 586.

15. Interrogation of Steven Avery, Two Rivers Police Dept. (Nov. 9, 2005), at https://www.youtube.com/watch?v=4T9k48VbUEI&feature=youtu.be.

16. Ibid.

17. Ibid.

18. Ibid.

19. Ibid.

20. Ibid. There was actually a great deal of evidence that someone else murdered Teresa Halbach and framed Steven Avery, with Brendan Dassey's conviction being an unintended result. (Assuming Avery was framed, the real killer could never have imagined that Dassey would also be convicted, given there was no physical evidence, eyewitness, or even an *accusation* against him.) Unfortunately, however, trial rules often prevent the jury from hearing evidence of third-party guilt. The most common justification for such truth-suppressing trial rules is judicial economy. See Michael D. Cicchini, "An Alternative to the Wrong-Person Defense," *George Mason University Civil Rights Law Journal* 24 (2013).

Chapter 17

1. Michael D. Cicchini and Joseph Easton, "Reforming the Law on Show-Up Identifications," *Journal of Criminal Law & Criminology* 100 (2010): 393 (quoting Timothy P. O'Toole and Giovanna Shay, "*Manson v. Brathwaite* Revisited: Towards a New Rule of Decision for Due Process Challenges to Eyewitness Identification Procedures," *Valparaiso University Law Review* 41 [2006]: 121).

2. Interrogation of Brendan Dassey, Mishicot High School (Feb. 27, 2006), 477, at http://www.stevenaverycase.org/wp-content/uploads/2016/02/Brendan-Dassey-Interview-at-School-Transcript-2006Feb27_text.pdf.

3. Ibid.

4. Interrogation of Brendan Dassey, Manitowoc County Sheriff's Dept. (Mar. 1, 2006), 570, at http://www.stevenaverycase.org/wp-content/uploads/2016/02/Brendan-Dassey-Interview-Transcript-2006Mar01_text.pdf.

5. Ibid.

6. Ibid., 595.

7. Ibid., 596–97.

8. Ibid., 597.

9. Ibid.

10. Ibid.

11. Ibid.

12. Ibid.

13. Ibid., 547.

14. Ibid., 668.

15. Ibid.

16. Ibid. (emphasis added).

17. Ibid.

Chapter 18

1. *State v. Dassey*, 827 N.W.2d 928, 2013 Wisc. App. LEXIS 85, *3.

2. Ibid., *4 (emphasis added).

3. Ibid.

4. Interrogation of Brendan Dassey, Mishicot High School (Feb. 27, 2006), 466, at http://www.stevenaverycase.org/wp-content/uploads/2016/02/Brendan-Dassey-Interview-at-School-Transcript-2006Feb27_text.pdf.

5. Ibid.

6. Interrogation of Brendan Dassey, Two Rivers Police Dept. (Feb. 27, 2006), 511, at http://www.stevenaverycase.org/wp-content/uploads/2016/02/Brendan-Dassey-Interview-at-Station-Transcript-2006Feb27_text.pdf.

7. Interrogation of Brendan Dassey, Manitowoc County Sheriff's Dept. (Mar. 1, 2006), 532, at http://www.stevenaverycase.org/wp-content/uploads/2016/02/Brendan-Dassey-Interview-Transcript-2006Mar01_text.pdf.

8. Ibid.

9. Ibid.

10. Ibid., 538.

11. Ibid., 611.

12. Ibid., 612.

13. Ibid.

14. Ibid., 613.

15. Ibid.

16. Ibid.

17. Ibid., 665.

18. Ibid.

19. Ibid., 676.

20. Ibid., 569.

21. Ibid., 570.

22. Ibid., 569–70 (emphasis added).

23. Ibid., 670.

24. Ibid.

25. Brief of Petitioner-Appellee Brendan Dassey, *Dassey v. Dittmann*, No. 16-3397 (U.S. Ct. App. 7th Cir., Dec. 6, 2016), 45.

Chapter 19

1. Interrogation of Brendan Dassey, Manitowoc County Sheriff's Dept. (Mar. 1, 2006), 597, at http://www.stevenaverycase.org/wp-content/uploads/2016/02/Brendan-Dassey-Interview-Transcript-2006Mar01_text.pdf.

2. Ibid., 640–41.

3. Brief of Petitioner-Appellee Brendan Dassey, *Dassey v. Dittmann*, No. 16-3397 (U.S. Ct. App. 7th Cir., Dec. 6, 2016), 16.

4. Interrogation of Brendan Dassey, Mishicot High School (Feb. 27, 2006), 471, at http://www.stevenaverycase.org/wp-content/uploads/2016/02/Brendan-Dassey-Interview-at-School-Transcript-2006Feb27_text.pdf.

5. Interrogation of Brendan Dassey, Two Rivers Police Dept. (Feb. 27, 2006), 492, at http://www.stevenaverycase.org/wp-content/uploads/2016/02/Brendan-Dassey-Interview-at-Station-Transcript-2006Feb27_text.pdf.

6. Interrogation of Brendan Dassey, Manitowoc County Sheriff's Dept., 629.

7. Ibid., 655.

8. Interrogation of Brendan Dassey, Mishicot High School, 473 (emphasis added).

9. Interrogation of Brendan Dassey, Two Rivers Police Dept., 496.

10. Ibid., 494.

11. Interrogation of Brendan Dassey, Manitowoc County Sheriff's Dept., 555 (emphasis added).

12. Ibid., 556 (emphasis added).

13. Ibid.

14. Ibid., 609.

15. Ibid.

16. Defendant Steven Avery's Memorandum on Brendan Dassey's Statements, *State v. Avery*, 2005-CF-381, Manitowoc County, Wis. (May 30, 2007) (emphasis added), at http://www.stevenaverycase.org/wp-content/uploads/2016/03/Defendants-Memo-on-Brendan-Dassey-Statements.pdf.

17. Brief of Defendant-Appellant, *State v. Dassey*, 2010AP3105-CR (Wis. Ct. App., Dec. 1, 2011), 86 (internal citations to the record omitted).

18. Interrogation of Brendan Dassey, Manitowoc County Sheriff's Dept., 672.

19. Ibid.

20. Ibid., 673.

21. Ibid.

Chapter 20

1. Brief of Petitioner-Appellee Brendan Dassey, *Dassey v. Dittmann*, No. 16-3397 (U.S. Ct. App. 7th Cir., Dec. 6, 2016), 37.

2. Ibid.

3. Ibid.

4. Interrogation of Brendan Dassey, Manitowoc County Sheriff's Dept. (Mar. 1, 2006), 613–14, at http://www.stevenaverycase.org/wp-content/uploads/2016/02/Brendan-Dassey-Interview-Transcript-2006Mar01_text.pdf.

5. Ibid., 614.

6. Ibid.

7. Ibid., 620.

8. Ibid., 620–21 (emphasis added).

9. Ibid., 668.

10. Ibid., 668–69.

Chapter 21

1. Wisconsin Supreme Court Rule (SCR) 20:3.6 (a).

2. SCR 20:3.6 (b) (2) (emphasis added).

3. *Making a Murderer*, dir. Moira Demos and Laura Ricciardi, aired December 18, 2015 (Los Angeles: Synthesis Films and Netflix).

4. Ibid.

5. SCR 20:3.6 (c) (2).

6. State's Response to Defendant's Motion to Dismiss—Pretrial Publicity, *State v. Avery*, 2005-CF-381, Manitowoc County, Wis. (July 5, 2006), at http://www.stevenaverycase.org/wp-content/uploads/2016/01/States-Response-to-Defendants-Motion-to-Dismiss-Pretrial-Publicity.pdf.

7. SCR 20:3.6 (d).

8. State's Response to Defendant's Motion to Dismiss—Pretrial Publicity, 1–2.

9. *Making a Murderer*.

10. Ibid.

11. Ibid. (emphasis added).

12. Ibid. (emphasis added).

13. Ibid.

14. Some attorney ethics rules are simply absurd. For example, ABA Model Rule 1.9, which has been adopted in most states, including Wisconsin, arguably prohibits lawyers (including defense lawyers and prosecutors) from discussing even the widely known *public* aspects of their *closed* cases. Most lawyers are not even aware this rule exists, and nearly all lawyers violate it on a daily basis. Most infractions go unreported, and lawyer disciplinary bodies prosecute violations on a highly selective basis. See Michael D. Cicchini, "On the Absurdity of Rule 1.9," *Vermont Law Review* 40 (2015): 69. I petitioned the Supreme Court of Wisconsin (SCOW) to change this rule but was opposed by the State Bar—an organization that supposedly works for its membership, the lawyers, yet actively seeks to suppress lawyer speech even with regard to widely available, public information. In a split decision, the court denied the petition. See Michael D. Cicchini, "All 'Riled' Up: SCOW Flops on Ethics Rule 1.9," *Wisconsin Law Journal* (August 3, 2016), at https://wislawjournal.com/2016/08/03/critics-corner-all-riled-up-scow-flops-on-ethics-rule-1-9/.

Chapter 22

1. *Burt v. Titlow*, 571 U.S. __ (2013) (Sotomayor, J., concurring) ("A defendant possesses the ultimate authority to determine her plea" and "a lawyer must

abide by his client's decision in this respect . . . after having provided the client with competent and fully informed advice, including an analysis of the risks that the client would face in proceeding to trial.").

2. See, for example, *State v. Cooks*, 726 N.W.2d 322, 325 (Wis. Ct. App. 2006), which held: "The State concedes, and we agree, that Cooks' trial counsel performed deficiently in this regard. Cooks' counsel had a duty to investigate the alibi witnesses Cook provided. We further conclude that such performance prejudiced Cooks' defense."

3. Brief of Defendant-Appellant, *State v. Dassey*, 2010AP3105-CR (Wis. Ct. App., Dec. 1, 2011), 55 (internal citations to the record omitted) (emphasis added).

4. Ibid., 57.

5. Brief of Petitioner-Appellee Brendan Dassey, *Dassey v. Dittmann*, No. 16-3397 (U.S. Ct. App. 7th Cir., Dec. 6, 2016), 49 (internal quotations omitted).

6. Brief of Defendant-Appellant, *State v. Dassey*, 58.

7. Ibid., 58–59.

8. Interrogation of Brendan Dassey, Sheboygan County Law Enforcement Center (May 13, 2006), 758, at http://www.stevenaverycase.org/wp-content/uploads/2016/02/Brendan-Dassey-Interview-Transcript-2006May13_text.pdf.

9. Ibid., 763.

10. Ibid., 764 (emphasis added).

11. Ibid., 770.

12. Ibid., 829.

13. Ibid., 856–57.

14. Ibid., 759–61.

15. Ibid.

16. Ibid.

17. Ibid.

18. Ibid., 775 (emphasis added).

19. Ibid., 776.

20. Ibid., 779.

21. Ibid., 771.

22. Ibid. (emphasis added).

23. Ibid., 773.

24. Ibid., 768.

25. Ibid.

26. Ibid. (emphasis added).

27. Ibid., 791 (emphasis added).

Chapter 23

1. Interrogation of Brendan Dassey, Sheboygan County Law Enforcement Center (May 13, 2006), 797, at http://www.stevenaverycase.org/wp-content/uploads/2016/02/Brendan-Dassey-Interview-Transcript-2006May13_text.pdf.

2. Ibid., 799.

3. Ibid., 800.

4. Ibid., 815–16 (emphasis added).

5. Ibid., 797.

6. Ibid., 822–23 (emphasis added).

7. Ibid.

8. Ibid., 829 (emphasis added).

9. Ibid., 861–62.

10. Brief of Defendant-Appellant, *State v. Dassey*, 2010AP3105-CR (Wis. Ct. App., Dec. 1, 2011), 60.

11. Ibid., 64 (hyphens added).

12. Brief of Petitioner-Appellee Brendan Dassey, *Dassey v. Dittmann*, No. 16-3397 (U.S. Ct. App. 7th Cir., Dec. 6, 2016), 49.

Chapter 24

1. Brief of Petitioner-Appellee Brendan Dassey, *Dassey v. Dittmann*, No. 16-3397 (U.S. Ct. App. 7th Cir., Dec. 6, 2016), 27.

2. Brief of Defendant-Appellant, *State v. Dassey*, 2010AP3105-CR (Wis. Ct. App., Dec. 1, 2011), 92.

3. Ibid., 97.

4. Ibid.

5. Ibid.

6. Ibid., 97–98.

7. Danielle E. Chojnacki, Michael D. Cicchini, and Lawrence T. White, "An Empirical Basis for the Admission of Expert Testimony on False Confessions," *Arizona State Law Journal* 40, no. 1 (2008): 32.

8. Brief of Defendant-Appellant, *State v. Dassey*, 93–94.

9. Ibid., 95.

10. Ibid., 90.

11. Ibid., 95.

12. Trial Transcript Day 1, *State v. Dassey*, Case No. 06-CF-88, Manitowoc County, Wis. (April 16, 2007), 20 (emphasis added) (reading Wis. Crim. Jury Instructions No. 140), at http://www.stevenaverycase.org/wp-content/uploads/2017/02/Dassey-Trial-Transcripts.pdf.

13. Michael D. Cicchini and Lawrence T. White, "Truth or Doubt? An Empirical Test of Criminal Jury Instructions," *University of Richmond Law Review* 50 (2016): 1154–56; Michael D. Cicchini and Lawrence T. White, "Testing the Impact of Criminal Jury Instructions on Verdicts: A Conceptual Replication," *Columbia Law Review Online* 117 (2017): 30–32. These two articles challenging Wisconsin's pattern jury instruction on the burden of proof have caused quite a stir among Wisconsin's prosecutors and trial judges—many of whom have reacted strongly and irrationally to our evidence and arguments. For some of their claims and arguments, see Michael D. Cicchini, "The Battle over the Burden of Proof: A Report from the Trenches," *University of Pittsburgh Law Review* 79 (2017), and Michael D. Cicchini and Lawrence T. White, "Educating Judges and Lawyers in Behavioral Research: A Case Study," *Gonzaga Law Review* 53 (2017). Despite this vehement opposition, at least twenty-two trial judges across the state have modified and improved Wisconsin's unconstitutional burden of proof instruction. See http://www.cicchinilawoffice.com/Wis_JI_140.html.

14. Cicchini and White, "Truth or Doubt?," 1157.

15. Cicchini and White, "Testing the Impact," 31–32.

16. *State v. Berube*, 286 P.3d 402, 411 (Wash. Ct. App. 2012).

17. Brief of Defendant-Appellant, *State v. Dassey*, 95.

Chapter 25

1. *Mincey v. Arizona*, 437 U.S. 385, 401 (1978).

2. Brief of Defendant-Appellant, *State v. Dassey*, 2010AP3105-CR (Wis. Ct. App., Dec. 1, 2011), 78 (citing cases from the Supreme Court of the United States and the Supreme Court of Wisconsin for the proposition that "special care" is required when analyzing juvenile confessions).

3. Ibid., 73–88.

4. *State v. Dassey*, 827 N.W.2d 928, ¶5 (Wis. Ct. App. 2013).

5. Ibid. (emphasis added) (two internal citations to case law omitted).

6. Brief of Petitioner-Appellee Brendan Dassey, *Dassey v. Dittmann*, No. 16-3397 (U.S. Ct. App. 7th Cir., Dec. 6, 2016), 41.

7. *State v. Dassey*, 827 N.W.2d 928, ¶5.

8. Brief of Petitioner-Appellee Brendan Dassey, *Dassey v. Dittmann*, 47.

9. Ibid.

10. Interrogation of Brendan Dassey, Mishicot High School (Feb. 27, 2006), 442–43 (emphasis added), at http://www.stevenaverycase.org/wp-content/uploads/2016/02/Brendan-Dassey-Interview-at-School-Transcript-2006Feb27_text.pdf.

11. *Making a Murderer*, dir. Moira Demos and Laura Ricciardi, aired December 18, 2015 (Los Angeles: Synthesis Films and Netflix).

Chapter 26

1. *Dassey v. Dittmann*, 2016 U.S. Dist. LEXIS 106971, *89 (emphasis added).
2. Ibid., *90.
3. Ibid., *75 (emphasis added) (internal quotations and citation omitted).
4. Ibid. (internal quotations and citation omitted).
5. Ibid., *91.
6. Ibid.
7. Ibid.
8. Ibid., *92.
9. Ibid., *92–93.
10. Ibid., *102.
11. Brief of Petitioner-Appellee Brendan Dassey, *Dassey v. Dittmann*, No. 16-3397 (U.S. Ct. App. 7th Cir., Dec. 6, 2016), 45.
12. *Dassey v. Dittmann*, 2016 U.S. Dist. LEXIS 106971, *110 (emphasis added).
13. Ibid.
14. Prosecutors often view constitutional safeguards as mere technicalities that stand in the way of the pursuit of justice. For example, before a motion hearing to suppress the sole piece of evidence against one of my clients, a prosecutor privately conceded to me that my analysis was correct, yet he was still opposing the motion to see what the trial judge would do. The prosecutor's decision paid off: the judge ruled in the state's favor and the ill-gotten evidence was deemed to be admissible at trial. This law-breaking mentality is common, and is even supported by published case law. For example, in the Fourth Amendment context, even when a court finds that there was, in fact, a constitutional violation, the ill-gotten evidence is rarely suppressed. Instead, courts typically rule that a defendant simply is not entitled to any remedy for the government's misconduct. For more on this, see Michael D. Cicchini, "An Economics Perspective on the Exclusionary Rule and Deterrence," *Missouri Law Review* 75 (2010): 459.

Chapter 27

1. *Dassey v. Dittmann*, 2016 U.S. Dist. LEXIS 106971, *89.
2. Prosecutors love to say that they are searching for the truth, but this is just word-game sophistry. First, claiming to be on the side of truth allows them to

paint defense lawyers as obfuscators who are merely trying to create doubt out of thin air. And second, "If one were asked to start from scratch and devise a system best suited to ascertaining the truth . . . [i]t is inconceivable that one would create a system bearing much resemblance to the criminal justice process we now have." Keith A. Findley, "Adversarial Inquisitions: Rethinking the Search for the Truth," *New York Law School Law Review* 56 (2011): 912. There are several reasons for this, including the state's tremendous advantage in financial resources over defendants, as well as the state's ability to control and even shape the evidence, including witness testimony.

3. *Dassey v. Dittmann*, 2016 U.S. Dist. LEXIS, *55.

4. Ibid.

5. Ibid., *57 (emphasis added).

6. Ibid. (emphasis added).

7. Ibid., *108.

8. Michael D. Cicchini, *Convicting Avery: The Bizarre Laws and Broken System behind Making a Murderer* (Amherst, NY: Prometheus Books, 2017), 175.

9. *Dassey v. Dittmann*, 2016 U.S. Dist. LEXIS 106971, *103.

Chapter 28

1. *Dassey v. Dittmann*, No. 16-3397, 48–50 (7th Cir. 2017) (three-judge panel) (emphasis added) (internal citations omitted).

2. Ibid., 55.

3. Ibid.

4. Ibid.

5. Ibid., 80–81 (emphasis added).

6. Ibid., 76–77.

7. Ibid., 99–100 (emphasis added).

8. Ibid., 59 (citing state's brief).

9. Ibid., 59.

10. Ibid., 103 (internal quotations omitted).

11. Ibid.

Chapter 29

1. *Dassey v. Dittmann*, 2016 U.S. Dist. LEXIS 106971, *57 (emphasis added).

2. Ibid., *108.

3. *Dassey v. Dittmann*, No. 16-3397, 49 (7th Cir. 2017) (three-judge panel) (internal citations omitted).

4. *Dassey v. Dittmann*, No. 16-3397 (7th Cir. 2017) (en banc).

5. Ibid., 4.

6. Ibid., 30 (emphasis added).

7. Ibid., 40 (Wood, Rovner, and Williams, dissenting).

8. Ibid., 57.

9. For salary information, and more on the judiciary's most recent money grab, see Patrick Marley, "Wisconsin Judges Seeking 16% Pay Hike," *Milwaukee Journal Sentinel* (January 8, 2017), at https://www.jsonline.com/story/news/politics/2017/01/08/wisconsin-judges-seeking-16-pay-hike/96217918/.

10. R. Lanier Anderson, "Friedrich Nietzsche: Critique of Religion and Morality," *Stanford Encyclopedia of Philosophy* (March 17, 2017) (discussing Nietzsche's famous saying that "God is dead"), at https://plato.stanford.edu/entries/nietzsche/#CritReliMora.

11. *Dassey v. Dittmann*, No. 16-3397, 40 (7th Cir. 2017) (en banc) (Wood, Rovner, and Williams, dissenting).

Chapter 30

1. Legal Information Institute s.v. "stare decisis" (March 2017), at https://www.law.cornell.edu/wex/stare_decisis.

2. *Payne v. Tennessee*, 501 U.S. 808, 827 (1991).

3. 466 U.S. 740 (1984).

4. Ibid., pp. 748-54 (internal quote marks and citations omitted) (emphasis added).

5. *Dassey v. Dittmann*, No. 16-3397, 36–48 (7th Cir. 2017) (three-judge panel) (internal citations omitted).

6. *Dassey v. Dittmann*, No. 16-3397, 31 (7th Cir. 2017) (en banc).

7. Ibid.

8. Ibid., 32 (internal quote marks omitted).

9. Ibid., 54–55 (Wood, Rovner, and Williams, dissenting).

10. Ambrose Bierce, *The Devil's Dictionary*, s.v. "precedent" (1911), at http://www.alcyone.com/max/lit/devils/p.html.

Chapter 31

1. Jacob Carpenter, "Wisconsin Pays Nation's Lowest Rate to Defend the Poor; Lawyers Say It's Time for a Raise," *Milwaukee Journal Sentinel* (May 24, 2017), at https://www.jsonline.com/story/news/investigations/2017/05/24/wisconsin-pays-nations-lowest-rate-defend-poor-lawyers-say-its-time-raise/342944001/.

Chapter 32

1. Michael D. Cicchini, "The New Miranda Warning," *Southern Methodist University Law Review* 65, no. 4 (2012): 933.

2. Ibid.

3. Ibid., 934.

4. In addition to minor substantive modifications, the footnotes that appeared in the original text have been omitted, and the formatting has also been changed. For the original text and the full article, visit the articles page of www.Cicchini-Law.com.

5. Cicchini, "The New Miranda Warning," 935–39.

Chapter 33

1. Interrogation of Brendan Dassey, Manitowoc County Sheriff's Dept. (Mar. 1, 2006), 527 (emphasis added), at http://www.stevenaverycase.org/wp-content/uploads/2016/02/Brendan-Dassey-Interview-Transcript-2006Mar01_text.pdf. This portion of the transcript is of the audio recording made while en route to the Manitowoc County Sheriff's Department, just minutes before commencing the in-house interrogation.

2. 466 U.S. 688 (1984).

3. For an example of bad plea bargaining advice in reverse, in *State v. Dillard*, 2014 WI 123, the defense lawyer incorrectly told the defendant that, if he went to trial and lost, he would be facing life imprisonment. The defendant relied on this advice and took a plea bargain to avoid such a fate. When it was later discovered that the advice was bad—that is, the defendant would not have faced life in prison had he lost at trial—the defendant moved to withdraw his plea. The Supreme Court of Wisconsin allowed the defendant to do so, contrary to the wishes of the prosecutor, the trial judge, and, amazingly, *three dissenting justices* on the court.

Chapter 34

1. Daniel D. Blinka, "The Daubert Standard in Wisconsin: A Primer," *Wisconsin Lawyer* 84, no. 3 (March 2011), at http://www.wisbar.org/NewsPublications/WisconsinLawyer/Pages/Article.aspx?Volume=84&Issue=3&ArticleID=2348.

2. Admin., "Drug Recognition Evaluator Passes Daubert Test for Admissibility of Expert Testimony," *On Point: Wisconsin State Public Defender* (April 13, 2016) (emphasis added), at http://www.wisconsinappeals.net/on-point-by-the-

wisconsin-state-public-defender/drug-recognition-evaluator-passes-daubert-test-for-admissibility-of-expert-testimony/.

3. Danielle E. Chojnacki, Michael D. Cicchini, and Lawrence T. White, "An Empirical Basis for the Admission of Expert Testimony on False Confessions," *Arizona State Law Journal* 40, no. 1 (2008): 1–45.

4. Wis. Stats. § 904.03 ("Although relevant, evidence may be excluded if its probative value is substantially outweighed by the danger of . . . confusion of the issues").

5. *State v. Haseltine*, 352 N.W.2d 673 (Wis. Ct. App. 1984) ("Under Wisconsin law, a witness may not testify that another mentally and physically competent witness is telling the truth.").

Chapter 35

1. Alan Pyke, "A Major Police Training Firm Just Abandoned the Dominant Method for Interrogating Suspects: It's a Big Deal—But How Big?," *Think Progress* (March 9, 2017), https://thinkprogress.org/reid-technique-false-confessions-db446bde1d0/.

2. Ibid.

3. Ibid. (quoting Eli Hager).

4. Eli Hager, "The Seismic Change in Police Interrogations," The Marshall Project (March 7, 2017), https://www.themarshallproject.org/2017/03/07/the-seismic-change-in-police-interrogations.

5. Ibid.

6. Christian A. Meissner, et al., "Accusatorial and Information-Gathering Interrogation Methods and their Effects on True and False Confessions: A Meta-Analytic Review," *Journal of Experimental Criminology* 10, no. 4 (2014): 459–86, https://works.bepress.com/christian_meissner/60/.

7. Pyke, "A Major Police Training Firm."

8. Ibid.

9. Ibid.

10. Ibid.

11. Keith A. Findley and Michael S. Scott, "The Multiple Dimensions of Tunnel Vision in Criminal Cases," *Wisconsin Law Review* (2006): 292.

Chapter 36

1. *State v. Avery*, 414 N.W.2d 319, *15 (Wis. Ct. App. 1987) (emphasis added).

2. Lawrence Solan, "Refocusing the Burden of Proof in Criminal Cases: Some Doubt about Reasonable Doubt," *Texas Law Review* 78 (1999): 108–9 (emphasis added).

3. *State v. Haseltine*, 352 N.W.2d 673 (Wis. Ct. App. 1984).

4. Danielle E. Chojnacki, Michael D. Cicchini, and Lawrence T. White, "An Empirical Basis for the Admission of Expert Testimony on False Confessions," *Arizona State Law Journal* 40, no. 1 (2008): 40–42.

5. Brief of Defendant-Appellant, *State v. Miller*, 2011AP901-CR (Wis. Ct. App., Aug. 10, 2011), 6–7.

6. *State v. Miller*, 2012 WI App. 68, ¶ 15.

7. Ibid., ¶ 16.

8. *Making a Murderer*, dir. Moira Demos and Laura Ricciardi, aired December 18, 2015 (Los Angeles: Synthesis Films and Netflix).

9. Ibid.

10. Interrogation of Brendan Dassey, Mishicot High School (Feb. 27, 2006), 440, at http://www.stevenaverycase.org/wp-content/uploads/2016/02/Brendan-Dassey-Interview-at-School-Transcript-2006Feb27_text.pdf.

Chapter 37

1. Petition for Writ of Certiorari, *Dassey v. Dittmann*, No. 17-___ (U.S. Supreme Court, Feb. 2018).

2. Ibid., 28 (internal citations omitted).

3. Ibid., 16.

4. Ibid., 31 (emphasis added).

5. Ibid.

6. Ibid., 1.

7. Ibid., 4.

8. Ibid., 30.

BIBLIOGRAPHY

Articles and Books

Admin. "Drug Recognition Evaluator Passes Daubert Test for Admissibility of Expert Testimony," *On Point: Wisconsin State Public Defender* (April 13, 2016). http://www.wisconsinappeals.net/on-point-by-the-wisconsin-state-public-defender/drug-recognition-evaluator-passes-daubert-test-for-admissibility-of-expert-testimony/.

Agar, James R. II. "The Admissibility of False Confession Expert Testimony." *Army Lawyer* 26 (1999).

Anderson, R. Lanier. "Friedrich Nietzsche: Critique of Religion and Morality." *Stanford Encyclopedia of Philosophy* (March 17, 2017). https://plato.stanford.edu/entries/nietzsche/#CritReliMora

Blinka, Daniel D. "The Daubert Standard in Wisconsin: A Primer." *Wisconsin Lawyer* 84, no. 3 (March 2011).

Carpenter, Jacob. "Wisconsin Pays Nation's Lowest Rate to Defend the Poor; Lawyers Say It's Time for a Raise." *Milwaukee Journal Sentinel* (May 24, 2017).

Cassell, Paul G., and Bret S. Hayman. "Police Interrogation in the 1990s: An Empirical Study of the Effects of Miranda." *UCLA Law Review* 43 (1996): 839.

Chang, Louise. "John Mark Karr and the False Confession: Why?" *WebMD*, Mental Health (August 29, 2006). https://www.webmd.com/mental-health/features/john-mark-karr-false-confession-why#1.

Chojnacki, Danielle E., Michael D. Cicchini, and Lawrence T. White. "An Empirical Basis for the Admission of Expert Testimony on False Confessions." *Arizona State Law Journal* 40, no. 1 (2008): 1.

Cicchini, Michael D. "All 'Riled' Up: SCOW Flops on Ethics Rule 1.9." *Wisconsin Law Journal* (August 3, 2016).

———. "An Alternative to the Wrong-Person Defense." *George Mason University Civil Rights Law Journal* 24, no. 1 (2013).

———. "An Economics Perspective on the Exclusionary Rule and Deterrence." *Missouri Law Review* 75 (2010): 459.

———. "The Battle over the Burden of Proof: A Report from the Trenches." *University of Pittsburgh Law Review* 79 (2017): 61.

———. "Combating Prosecutor Misconduct in Closing Arguments." *Oklahoma Law Review* 70, no. 3 (2018).

———. *Convicting Avery: The Bizarre Laws and Broken System behind Making a Murderer*. Amherst, NY: Prometheus Books, 2017.

———. "The New Miranda Warning." *Southern Methodist University Law Review* 65 (2012): 911.

———. "The Non-Recommendation Recommendation (and Other Government Bullshit)." *The Legal Watchdog* (August 17, 2013).

———. "On the Absurdity of Rule 1.9." *Vermont Law Review* 40 (2015):69

Cicchini, Michael D., and Joseph Easton. "Reforming the Law on Show-Up Identifications." *Journal of Criminal Law & Criminology* 100 (2010): 381

Cicchini, Michael D., and Lawrence T. White. "Convictions Based on Character: An Empirical Test of Other-Acts Evidence." *Florida Law Review* 70 (2018).

———. "Educating Judges and Lawyers in Behavioral Research: A Case Study." *Gonzaga Law Review* 53, no. 1 (2018)

———. "Testing the Impact of Criminal Jury Instructions on Verdicts: A Conceptual Replication." *Columbia Law Review Online* 117 (2017): 22.

———. "Truth or Doubt? An Empirical Test of Criminal Jury Instructions." *University of Richmond Law Review* 50 (2016): 1139.

Domanico, Anthony, Michael D. Cicchini, and Lawrence T. White. "Overcoming Miranda: A Content Analysis of the Miranda Portion of Police Interrogations." *Idaho Law Review* 49 (2012): 1.

Findley, Keith A. "Adversarial Inquisitions: Rethinking the Search for the Truth." *New York Law School Law Review* 56 (2011): 912.

Findley, Keith A., and Michael S. Scott. "The Multiple Dimensions of Tunnel Vision in Criminal Cases." *Wisconsin Law Review* (2006): 291.

Hager, Eli. "The Seismic Change in Police Interrogations." *The Marshall Project* (March 7, 2017).

Kassin, Saul M. "The Psychology of Confession Evidence." *American Psychologist* 52, no. 3 (1997): 221–33.

Saul M. Kassin, Richard A. Leo, Christian A. Meissner, Kimberly D. Richman, Lori H. Colwell, Amy-May Leach, and Dana La Fon. "Police Interviewing and Interrogation: A Self-Report Survey of Police Practices and Beliefs." *Law & Human Behavior* 31, no. 4 (2007): 381–400.

Kassin, Saul M., and Karlyn McNall. "Police Interrogations and Confessions: Communicating Promises and Threats by Pragmatic Implication." *Law & Human Behavior* 15, no. 3 (1991): 233–51.

Leo, Richard A. "Inside the Interrogation Room." *Journal of Criminal Law &* *Criminology* 86 (1996): 266.

Marley, Patrick. "Wisconsin Judges Seeking 16% Pay Hike." *Milwaukee Journal Sentinel* (January 8, 2017).

Meissner, Christian A., Allison D. Redlich, Stephen W. Michael, Jacqueline R. Evans, Catherine R. Camilletti, Sujeeta Bhatt, and Susan Brandon. "Accusatorial and Information-Gathering Interrogation Methods and Their Effects on True and False Confessions: A Meta-Analytic Review." *Journal of Experimental Criminology* 10, no. 4 (2014): 459–86.

Nesterak, Evan. "Coerced to Confess: The Psychology of False Confessions." *The Psych Report* (October 21, 2014).

Ogletree, Charles J. "Are Confessions Really Good for the Soul? A Proposal to Mirandize Miranda." *Harvard Law Review* 100 (1987): 1826.

O'Toole, Timothy P., and Giovanna Shay. "*Manson v. Brathwaite* Revisited: Towards a New Rule of Decision for Due Process Challenges to Eyewitness Identification Procedures." *Valparaiso University Law Review* 41 (2006); 109.

Pyke, Alan. "A Major Police Training Firm Just Abandoned the Dominant Method for Interrogating Suspects: It's a Big Deal—But How Big?" *Think Progress* (March 9, 2017).

Russano, Melissa B., Christian A. Meissner, Fadia M. Narchet, and Saul M. Kassin. "Investigating True and False Confessions within a Novel Experimental Paradigm." *Psychological Science* 16, no. 6 (2005): 481–86.

Softley, Paul. *Police Interrogation: An Observational Study in Four Police Stations.* Home Office Research Unit Report 28. London: HMSO, 1980.

Solan, Lawrence. "Refocusing the Burden of Proof in Criminal Cases: Some Doubt about Reasonable Doubt." *Texas Law Review* 78 (1999): 105.

Strauss, Marcy. "The Sounds of Silence: Reconsidering the Invocation of the Right to Remain Silent under Miranda." *William & Mary Bill of Rights Journal* 17 (2009): 773.

Thompson, Sandra Guerra. "Evading Miranda: How Seibert and Patane Failed to "Save" Miranda." *Valparaiso University Law Review* 40 (2006): 645.

Weisselberg, Charles D. "Mourning Miranda." *California Law Review* 96 (2008): 1519.

Wiseman, Christine, and Michael Tobin. *Criminal Practice and Procedure* Wisconsin Practice Series. Second edition. Eagan, MN: West, 2008.

Court Documents

Brief of Defendant-Appellant, *State v. Dassey*, 2010AP3105-CR (Wis. Ct. App., Dec. 1, 2011).

Brief of Defendant-Appellant, *State v. Miller*, 2011AP901-CR (Wis. Ct. App., Aug. 10, 2011).

Brief of Petitioner-Appellee Brendan Dassey, *Dassey v. Dittmann*, No. 16-3397 (U.S. Ct. App. 7th Cir., Dec. 6, 2016).

Defendant Steven Avery's Memorandum on Brendan Dassey's Statements, *State v. Avery*, 2005-CF-381, Manitowoc County, Wis. (May 30, 2007).

Interrogation of Brendan Dassey, Manitowoc County Sheriff's Dept. (Mar. 1, 2006).

Interrogation of Brendan Dassey, Marinette County Squad Car (Nov. 6, 2005).

Interrogation of Brendan Dassey, Mishicot High School (Feb. 27, 2006).

Interrogation of Brendan Dassey, Sheboygan County Law Enforcement Center (May 13, 2006).

Interrogation of Brendan Dassey, Two Rivers Police Dept. (Feb. 27, 2006).

Marinette County Sheriff's Department Supplemental Report Investigative Division, Case No. 05-4120 (Jan. 31, 2016) [*sic*].

Petition for Writ of Certiorari, *Dassey v. Dittmann*, No. 17-___ (U.S. Supreme Court, Feb. 2018).

State's Response to Defendant's Motion to Dismiss—Pretrial Publicity, *State v. Avery*, 2005-CF-381, Manitowoc County, Wis. (July 5, 2006).

Trial Transcript Day 1, *State v. Dassey*, Case No. 06-CF-88, Manitowoc County, Wis. (April 16, 2007).

Trial Transcript Day 4, *State v. Dassey*, Case No. 06-CF-88, Manitowoc County, Wis. (April 19, 2007).

Trial Transcript Day 5, *State v. Dassey*, Case No. 06-CF-88, Manitowoc County, Wis. (April 20, 2007).

Cases

Burt v. Titlow, 571 U.S. ___ (2013).

Dassey v. Dittmann, 2016 U.S. Dist. LEXIS 106971, 201 F. Supp. 3d 963.

Dassey v. Dittmann, No. 16-3397, 860 F.3d 933 (7th Cir. 2017) (three-judge panel).

Dassey v. Dittmann, No. 16-3397, 877 F.3d 297 (7th Cir. 2017) (en banc).

McClellan v. State, 193 N.W.2d 711 (Wis. 1972).

Mincey v. Arizona, 437 U.S. 385 (1978).

Miranda v. Arizona, 384 U.S. 436 (1966).

Payne v. Tennessee, 501 U.S. 808 (1991).

State v. Avery, 414 N.W.2d 319 (Wis. Ct. App. 1987).

State v. Berube, 286 P.3d 402 (Wash. Ct. App. 2012).

State v. Cooks, 726 N.W.2d 322 (Wis. Ct. App. 2006).

State v. Dassey, 827 N.W.2d 928, 2013 Wisc. App. LEXIS 85.

State v. Deets, 187 Wis. 2d 630 (Ct. App. 1994).

State v. Dillard, 2014 WI 123.

State v. Haseltine, 352 N.W.2d 673 (Wis. Ct. App. 1984).

State v. Jerrell C.J., 283 Wis.2d 145 (2005).

State v. Locke, 837 N.W.2d 178 (Wis. Ct. App. 2013).

State v. Miller, 2012 WI App. 68.

State v. Saeger, 2010 WI App. 135.

Strickland v. Washington, 466 U.S. 688 (1984).

United States v. Rutledge, 900 F.2d 1127 (7th Cir. 1990).

United States v. Yusuff, 96 F.3d 982 (7th Cir. 1996).

Welsh v. Wisconsin, 466 U.S. 740 (1984).

ABOUT THE AUTHOR

Michael D. Cicchini is a criminal defense attorney and author. He practices law in Kenosha, Wisconsin, about two hours south of Manitowoc where the events in *Making a Murderer* unfolded. As a defense lawyer, he has obtained pretrial dismissals and has won jury trials in dozens of cases, including conspiracy to commit murder, robbery, sexual assault, substantial battery, child abuse, fraud, and other serious felonies. He has also litigated Miranda and confession issues at both the pretrial and trial stages of the criminal process.

Based on his case outcomes, Cicchini was named a "top young lawyer" in Wisconsin by *Super Lawyers* and *Milwaukee* magazines from 2006 through 2010, and a "top 100 trial lawyer" in Wisconsin by the American Trial Lawyers (now the National Trial Lawyers) in 2009. He has also been named a "top criminal defense lawyer" in Wisconsin by other organizations.

In addition to practicing criminal defense, Cicchini writes extensively on legal matters including Miranda rights, interrogation tactics, and false confessions. Most significantly, he has published nineteen law review articles and three other books on criminal law and procedure. He has written for the *Wisconsin Law Journal*, the *Marquette University Law School Faculty Blog*, and the *Criminal Element* blog. He also writes about criminal law and other topics at *The Legal Watchdog* blog, which he founded in 2010.

Cicchini earned his J.D., *summa cum laude* and first in his class, from Marquette University Law School in Milwaukee. Before law school he earned an MBA degree (Marquette) and CPA certificate (Illinois) and lived a simpler existence crunching numbers in the corporate world. Visit www.CicchiniLaw.com for more information, including the full text of his law review articles and links to his columns, blog posts, and other books.

ABOUT THE AUTHOR

Also by Michael D. Cicchini:

Convicting Avery: The Bizarre Laws and Broken System behind "Making a Murderer" (2017)

Tried and Convicted: How Police, Prosecutors, and Judges Destroy Our Constitutional Rights (2012)

But They Didn't Read Me My Rights! Myths, Oddities, and Lies about Our Legal System (with Amy Kushner, 2010)